Achieving Success in Inner City Schools

A Guide for New and Seasoned Teachers

Christina D. Edwards, Ed.D.

Achieving Success in Inner City Schools
A Guide for New and Seasoned Teachers

Copyright © 2018 by Christina D. Edwards, Ed.D.

All rights reserved. No part of this book may be reproduced or transmitted in any form or by any means without written permission of the author.

ISBN 978-0-578-41307-5

This book is dedicated to every student I have ever taught, and to every educator who has a passion to change the world one student at a time.
You rock!
&
Most importantly, thank you God for using me for your benefit.

Contents

Preface 1
Introduction 5
1 The Purpose 9
2 (How to Really)
   Build Strong Teacher-Student Relationships 19
3 Classroom Management that Boosts Student
   Achievement 61
4 Teaching Methods and Strategies 99
5 Working Successfully with your Principal 137
6 Building the Bridge to Parental Engagement 153
Further Suggested Reading 169
Bibliography 171

Preface

MY BOOK WRITING journey started a couple of years back. I had graduated with my doctorate years earlier but questioned my next feat. Being a published author had always been a desire of mine; however, writing an article was more of my idea but definitely not a book! But, the more I worked with teachers within my district and attended trainings and workshops near and far, the more I realized I had something worth saying, and it was only fair to students and teachers to share the wealth.

If I didn't know how to do anything else, I knew how to teach. But, I later realized that teaching was not even half the battle. The relationships and the impact on the school and community were even more important than the academics. Students and I always seemed to connect and although some gave me pure hell, I had a soft spot in my heart for them. Was it always like this? Most of the time. I had struggles as every teacher had, but I considered them little hiccups and used them to better myself and learn and grow from them.

How blessed am I to come from a family full of educators! While finishing up this book, I summoned my grandmother, auntie, and mama to meet with me on many occasions to share their own experiences as former educators within the same district I was once employed. I needed feedback and their insight into my manuscript. For several Saturdays, we convened; Oh!

What dialogue we had over blueberry waffles, hash browns, eggs, bacon, and grits! It's amazing how we shared similar stories even with many decades of experience among us. Throughout their shared memories of challenges, there was always a victory story that followed. They were all retired, but even my more current accounts triggered memories of their experiences. Although my directions for my family was to read over the manuscript and evaluate it, it was hard to stick to the script! Our conversations of students, colleagues, and situations took us hours away from where we were supposed to be, but eventually, we got it done. They have supported and encouraged me to keep going. Thank you, Auntie (Chandra Ponder), Grandma (Dr. Jacquelyn Ponder), and especially mama (Yvette Edwards). I am grateful for your guidance, suggestions, and feedback that helped me through this process.

Why a book that focuses on the inner city? There were some who thought I should broaden my title and thought I might limit myself. However, I chose to focus on inner-city schools because it is my heart. I understand the defeats and triumphs. All schools are not treated equally primarily due to their zip codes.

The truth is a simple multicultural or classroom management course will not train teachers properly. The books I thought I should read to prepare me for inner city teaching didn't address my need. Although some educators have turned away, there is beauty in the inner city and many successes. Teachers can't turn students away and choose who we want in our classrooms; we have to learn to make it work and that is exactly what I did. Some have struggled, while others found their methods. This guide is full of my effective methods, from dealing with the personalities of various school leaders to building relationships with students. My desire is for you to see the flower that may be growing out of the cement and not give up on it, despite all that may deter you. I want you to go to work daily and give it all you've got while still stopping to smell the roses and hearing the birds chirp. There

PREFACE

is so much time, dedication, frustrations, and celebrations that occur and it's easy to lose yourself and forget to enjoy life. Don't! The goal of this book is to support you. I want to help you avoid the pitfalls I've witnessed and experienced. My hope is you read this book, and use it to sharpen yourselves professionally and personally.

Although I have targeted the inner city, the strategies and ideas in this book can be adapted and applied to any school setting.

For new teachers of the inner city, you've got this! Ain't nothing to it but to do it! May you take this book to heart and do your damn thing!

For seasoned educators who are getting sick and tired, sometimes retreating is necessary. Revisit your "why", and return refreshed!

For seasoned educators wanting to avoid burnout, revisit your strategies to determine what works and what doesn't. As the saying goes, "work smarter, not harder."

Everything in this book, which I call your guide, was written with you in mind. May this book (re)ignite your fire and be as beneficial to you as it has been to me.

Ready? Aim. Fire!

Best regards,
Christina D. Edwards, Ed. D.
Icoachteachers.com

Introduction

Every child deserves a champion — an adult who will never give up on them, who understands the power of connection and insists that they become the best that they can possibly be.

—RITA PIERSON

THIS NATION IS in dire need of retaining great teachers, strong administrators, and effective leaders of public education in the inner city. We need game changers; educators who will go above and beyond the call of duty to make certain that the children we touch daily won't be labeled as throwaways. We need to make sure that we, as educators, don't take one child for granted, no matter where their neighborhood school is located. There are lawmakers, who have never stepped foot in an inner city classroom, as instructional captains, nor do they have a sufficient understanding of the intricate parts of what makes a school effective. However, they become our district leaders and the decision holders of our schools and make insubstantial policies that focus on personal agendas, and monetary and political gains that subsequently are the dehumanizing effects of bureaucracy; despite, we cannot let our children, especially of the inner city, fall by the wayside. We need zero excuses as to why our students aren't achieving as other students in more prominent areas. Regardless of the challenges within and outside of our classrooms, our students deserve a good education. A Buddhist proverb once stated,

> "If a seed of a lettuce will not grow,
> we do not blame the lettuce.
> Instead, the fault lies with us
> for not having nourished the seed properly."

In the same way, no matter what the policies are on the outside, we can no longer allow excuses to dictate the learning growth of our children.

What is inner city? It is defined as the area near the center of a city, especially when associated with social and economic problems where mostly poor minorities live. In America, inner city connotes to low socioeconomic status, welfare, crime-soiled communities, uneducated and incapable, unemployed, broken, single-family homes filled with poor blacks, Hispanics and poverty-stricken whites. A dumping ground. A statistic. There are innumerable stigmas about inner city schools that have festered and spread over decades. When it comes to the educational system, some consider inner city schools to house incompetent students, teachers, and their leaders. It has been said by some that schools don't improve and are full of low achievers; they [schools] lack resources; students can't and don't learn. It has also been stated that student learning is stagnant and parents are the least involved and simply don't care about their children's education. Movies such as Lean on Me, Dangerous Minds, Stand and Deliver, To Sir with Love, Coach Carter, and Freedom Riders, to name a few, give a grim portrayal of the day-to-day lives for at-risk students at school and home. Many people I encounter often inquire if the movies authentically mirror inner

INTRODUCTION

city schools. "Is this what you deal with every day?" "Do children live in these conditions?" "Are children really this 'bad'?" There are some who are not able to fathom teaching kids "like this"; they will never understand what we do, why we do it, and how we do it. Some inner city schools can be more alarming than others, but the gist of it is very real. True educators of the inner city experience this firsthand. Unfortunately, I've had students who've come to school with court-monitored ankle bracelets; some have had their probation officers visit the school to monitor their progress. Some students became middle and high school dropouts, while others ended up on the news for various offenses, including murder. Some of my former students have had babies as early as the sixth grade, and the cycle repeated a few years later before exiting high school. However, through all my battles, and there have been a gamut of them, I have experienced some of my most memorable students and parents; some have been high-achieving high school and college graduates, who graduated with honors with full scholarships to colleges they never imagined or even knew existed years prior. I've had some of the strongest parents as their child's biggest supporters. I've witnessed students that, despite the odds, have beaten the unfortunate hand they were dealt. I left with an imprint that has changed the way I will forever view inner city children, and in return, I'm confident that I have left a portrait of what an effective, attentive, thoughtful, and strong teacher looks like and that this positive attitude has had a greater impact on them than their experiences with teachers who were totally disconnected and should have found another profession long ago. Their stories are my fuel, my reasons; I take them with me often. Their stories make what I do worth it. The world has cast out *these* children, like a piece of scrap paper waiting to be vacuumed, then dumped. So, let me make this clear to you, the reader.

Dear Teacher,

Great teachers are greatly needed. *These* children, our future, need you. Ironically, right now, many of them are unaware of their need for you. But, if you haven't been told lately, you are appreciated for all you do!

Sincerely,
Your fellow colleague

There are many teachers that have taken up vacancies for a salary; there are others who are dedicated and determined to giving their all; however, more great teachers of the inner city are needed.

This is a manual; a real manual that will ensure your success while teaching in the inner city. Actually, this is more than a manual; consider this your bible, your saving grace. You can thank me at the end of your successful school year and the years to come. This manual will make life easier while battling with inner city students, administration, the politics of education, parents, and all the great things that come along in the world of urban education.

The Purpose

I HAVE SOME QUESTIONS for you. Why did you become a teacher? Truly, of all the professions available, why was this the *chosen* one? Was inner city a first choice? Second? Was it any choice? What do you hope to accomplish as an inner city teacher? Are you here to fulfill a teacher education program obligation? Most importantly, is your heart really in it to win it? Take a moment to reflect on those questions.

Reflect: Think about your philosophy of education. You, if not already, have written your purpose for why you are a teacher. In essence, this is your core belief, your purpose, your guiding principle of your role as teacher. Although you may think you have completed your philosophy, you actually haven't! It should be a work in progress and will be adjusted throughout your professional career as you gain more experiences. Initially, I took the time to *really* write my, what I considered, stellar piece, I was so into it; however, I truly didn't understand how meaningful this was to my future career. Was it supposed to do something for or to you? Did my core belief and purpose really matter once I entered the classroom and left undergrad? It was years into my career before I rediscovered my philosophy on my computer's hard drive; I hadn't even remembered what I wrote. However, when I read it, it suddenly re-energized me. I wrote this? When I had graduated, I was so excited about my journey ahead that I really poured my soul into it, but throughout the years, my momentum was submerged under stress, aggravation, and frustration of the day-to-day of teacher life. After rereading my once-prized paper, my mission was revitalized! I edited it, memorized it, and posted it! My philosophy, although once null and void, became my mission personified. Sometimes, you may feel like your work is unrecognized and unappreciated and in fact, that may be possible; sometimes, you will have to encourage yourself and remind yourself why you chose this route. Post your philosophy on your wall. Memorize it. Live by it. Own it! Take the time to modify yours and begin writing it on the following page.

THE PURPOSE

name

philosophy of education:

Figure 1

Around my fourth year of teaching, I considered myself still new to the profession but a well-experienced classroom teacher. I can recall sitting in a faculty meeting one afternoon, and the presenter, a former teacher who worked in central office, stated that if teachers weren't going home every day butt-tired and beaten down, dragging in the morning and afternoon, then we weren't doing our jobs right; we were failing our students. I'm sure my face revealed how I really felt about what she was saying. I begged her pardon! Anything she said after that I don't recall, because I quickly tuned her out and negated anything that came along with that. The truth was, I was tired as any teacher would be after teaching adolescence who were full-grown adults one hour and babies the next, but her stance on it was completely not relatable to me. But I noticed that some teachers were butt-tired just as she described. I wasn't to that extent, led alone every day. Did that mean I wasn't doing something right and they were? Did I have to stay at school until eight each day to make a meaningful impact on my students? Were my students suffering at my discretion? After much consideration and reflection, my conclusion was finalized. No, I don't think so! So, let me say this, if you go home and arrive each morning as that lady described, don't put this book down. If you are sick and tired of being sick and tired, don't put this book down. If you are new to the field and entering an inner city school, don't put this book down. If you are a seasoned educator and need reenergizing, don't put this book down. This guide definitely has something for you.

I must admit I have gone to work feeling trampled at times, and working in inner city, you will (this is my disclaimer). There will be days when you'll question your own sanity. You'll question your purpose in this profession. You may dislike or even despise your job at some point. You may get to work before your scheduled time but sit in the school's parking lot to get your mind together until the absolute last minute before checking in for the day. You'll get sick and tired of the students, parents, colleagues, administration, the damn building, the damn books, the damn walls, even the damn street where your damn school sits. You may even begin to look into other career paths while visiting various websites on your lunch break or planning, heck, you may glance at career pages during class time. You may begin to look into your sick leave bank and start planning your absences, your maternity/paternity leave, or surgeries you can schedule and expedite them in a last-ditch effort to just not be at work. You may even begin looking into retirement to determine how many years you have left before you can give it all up. You'll be on an emotional roller coaster, but does it truly have to be this way? I am guilty of doing most of these at one point of time or another. However, looking back, I believe there is nothing more rewarding than earning your stripes, and after 10 years in a large urban school district, all my stripes were well deserved. When I speak about inner city, I definitely have stories to tell and the experience that made it not only work, but made it a success! But wait, I didn't introduce myself. Who am I? How did I come to write this manual? Do I really have the experience and accolades to speak on this topic? Why, yes. I am a former seasoned teacher, mentor, and coach; a former director of an alternative center, and presently self employed with iCoachTeachers Educational Consultants. I come from a bloodline of educators: retired principals and assistant principals, educational specialists, directors, teachers, para-professionals, and coaches. As a child, if I was asked what I wanted to be when I grew up, everyone in the world would have replied, "a teacher." Some of your stories may have different beginnings but, ultimately, we all arrived at the same destination. It seemed only natural for me to join the world of education and when I taught it was my innate ability, but no one, not my family, the two-week new teacher orientation I attended offered from the district as a new hire, nor the thousands of dollars of college tuition, and hundreds of hours of student teaching and observations/practicums can prepare you for actually entering the classroom of this particular sector and experiencing your OWN class.

I can recall my first interview at the local job fair. The school I desired was in the northern part of the district. It was considered to have "better" students, less discipline problems, more technology, and "better" teachers. Students did not eat on free or reduced lunches, and the school was surrounded by expensive homes, two-parent households, and students who were well traveled. The problem for me was, there was a very low turnover rate for teachers in that school. They maintained a full staff who were like magnets; they weren't going anywhere anytime soon unless it was to retire. Instead of school representatives, there was an empty table which displayed their school's name—empty; I was flabbergasted when I discovered there were no openings, but I kept searching for another one of the "good schools." As I continued to roam around the auditorium, I stumbled across a familiar school that was located on the south side of town; it had a reputation, like most schools on the south side of town. I was hesitant to approach the table at first, but I forged ahead. At the table sat two representatives, a male and female. I handed them my resume and the interview began. I had just graduated in May, here it was June, and August would be soon approaching; it was time to bring home the bacon. I'm sure I stumbled over my responses due to the flying butterflies that filled my stomach, but that didn't stop anything. Ultimately, I was offered the job and hired on the spot. That quickly? Was I that good, or were they that desperate? That could have been a red flag, or not, but I was too excited and shared my news with family and friends. Some shared in my excitement. Others were concerned with my choice of school. Could I thrive in such an environment? "Are you sure you want to teach there? Do you really know where that school sits?"

"Should I rethink this?" I thought. Did they shake me up a little? Yes, but just a little. A *friend* assured me that I would not even survive after the first year! I did 10. Successfully. Entering the building felt like I was finally growing up. Straight out of college. I graduated in May and here I was starting my career three months later and ready for what was to come. Most everyone was welcoming. Here is this twenty-something-year-old girl coming to teach children who many labeled as "bad" kids from the hood, poverty stricken, with a lack of home training and respect for authority. I heard two other colleagues, who worked at the school look, at me hesitantly and questioned if I knew what I was getting myself into. I was ready, though. People's doubt became my ammunition to not only conquer this journey I was embarking on, but to conquer it like nobody's business. Besides, I was a product of this school system; I was ready. It seemed like a new generation even though I had graduated high school five years prior. I entered through the metal detector; my mission had begun. My first year, I shed a few tears. Deadlines, meetings, unrealistic and irrelevant requirements were overwhelming. I needed air; my desires to teach were being suffocated. This was part of the program that my professors lightly touched on in undergrad, but certainly not in depth; experiencing it was another story. Was I really ready for this? Is this really the career path I wanted? I had to catch my rhythm, or I would drown fast. After a few shed tears and calls to my mother for help, I found my niche and finally moved to the beat of my own drum. Fast forward ten years later, I had become Teacher of the Year and the district's semi-finalist; I was featured on the cover of a popular local magazine where I was recognized as an exceptional teacher; I was the recipient of numerous awards and had received much recognition for student achievements. I became an appointed teacher mentor and leader to newly hired and seasoned teachers, grade-level chairman, content department lead, and a host of other titles and recognitions, and because I had demonstrated exemplary abilities, I had been appointed professional development facilitator and trainer on various topics within and outside the state.

This is my guide to you. I know what I'm talking about. I've lived it. I've experienced it. People will look at you sideways when you tell them the area where you work. It's all right. Inner city teaching is challenging; there will be days where you want to give up; some days you would rather take a sick day than be at work. It happens to the best of us, but hold your own. It is difficult, but if you do it correctly, you, too, will have success stories after success stories. More than few. Some inner city children don't have an Amen corner; you will be their advocate, their voice. You will wear a gamut of hats, from counselor, to nurse, to mom or dad, to mentor, to coach, to what you were originally hired for—to be their teacher. Don't lose focus; don't lose your passion; you may be the only person that child has who cares. You will change lives—negatively or positively. If I entertained others' negativity towards my profession and the area in which I chose to work, I'm sure my path would be much different. The only way you will thrive is if you are in. Are you all in?

Teachers take on much responsibility with their students. Parents *should* be the ones to teach their child standard manners and discipline. They *should* make sure their child is completing homework, daily assignments and projects. When there is a project, you *should* not have to purchase the material for them; it is their project, after all. Respecting authority *should* be a no-brainer. Parents *should*; students *should*; they *should*; I totally believe this; however, what happens when this is not the case for some of your past, present, and future students? The responsibility is on the school, on you. What is not taught at home, you have to teach them; don't fail our children. The pressure is on. On several occasions, I have witnessed students do such things as walk in the middle of a conversation, not hold the door for the person entering behind them, or interrupt a conversation by abruptly speaking. Unfortunately, I've witnessed educators make a fuss about what the students did instead of making it a teachable moment. People *do* because they haven't been taught what *not* to do. You will teach them that when people are conversing to walk around them and not in between; teach them to hold the door for the person walking behind them, and to say "excuse me" before interrupting a conversation. This is part of our job that *they* didn't tell us about in coursework. Are you in?

Schools in the inner city are not one-dimensional and there is not a simple remedy. The characteristics of inner city are distinctive from other areas. Keep in mind that you aren't Superman. So, entering in with an "I'm going to save *these* children" attitude won't work. In fact, you'll run yourself dry. There are a myriad challenges that are not prevalent in more suburban schools, so prepare yourself by becoming knowledgable of the area in which you plan to teach. However, when all intricate parts work together cohesively, and when the primary focus is student achievement mixed with consistency and high expectations, schools can perform at their maximum ability. All in all, only the strong will survive. You will have an abundance of roles and responsibilities that will be overbearing, but at the end of the day, you will have impacted so many lives, and that is more valuable than anything. Are you committed?

My beliefs are grounded in research, logic, personal experiences, as well as the accounts of past, present, and former educators.

(How to Really) Build Strong Teacher-Student Relationships

Students don't care how much you know until they know how much you care.

—ANONYMOUS

IT WASN'T EVEN mid-year yet, and four teachers in my building had already bitten the dust and resigned in search of other professions. As a matter of fact, stories like this were very common among neighboring schools. Why were teachers leaving in droves, especially so early in the game, and who would be the next to leave? Teachers were sick and tired of being sick and tired; the burnout was evident. Students weren't respecting their authority, and students were not putting any effort in completing, or even starting classwork or homework assignments. As much as I thought about following in my colleagues' footsteps, I couldn't. I knew I couldn't save all my students, but I could make a powerful impact on more than a few, and I was more than willing. Plus, with a mortgage, car note, and student loans in heavy monthly rotation, I needed the income!

What were the underlying issues? Where was the motivation of the students, teachers, and faculty? What paradigm shift needed to occur to save students from self-destructive behavior and to retain our good, strong teachers? Did students not understand they are our future and we are the pathmakers to their success? Students who have a positive relationship with their teaches are more likely to respect their authority, to exhibit positive behavior towards that teacher, and to enhance the learning experience. Canter (1997) points out that we all can recall classes in which we did not try very hard because we didn't like our teachers. This should remind us how important it is to have strong, positive relationships with our students.

Building positive relationships with students is about meeting students where they are, making a genuine effort to understand them, and taking the time to develop connections with them. Too often, I've witnessed new and even experienced teachers leave the teaching profession way too soon. "These kids are too much; they don't listen." "I can't do this any longer." "This is for the birds!" To be honest, I understood—a few. I sympathized with some, but not all. Teaching in this particular sector is hard; it's no joke! Some teachers are cut out to do this while others are not built for it. However, some people cause their own storms then get mad when it rains, and for some, it poured. Don't be one of those people. In order to reach children, they must believe you care. It's all about building positive teacher-student relationships. Genuine relationships. This is the foundation to being successful in the classroom. Therefore, we must take special care to let our students know from day one that we want them there—and that we are eager to get to know them, academically and personally, because we know that who we are affects how we interact with others and how we learn (Brown-Jeffy and Cooper 2011). It is pertinent to do this from the beginning. Now, don't get me wrong, you'll still go through challenges, but the challenges will be far less than what your colleagues may experience. I adopted the mind frame of *"my students, my children"* and put away words such as *"those students, those children."* Let's reflect: Characteristically, how are you as a teacher? What lasting impression do you hope students remember about you for years to come? If a group of your students, past and present, were asked by a stranger or maybe a board member to describe you as a teacher, would students have nice things to say? Or negative? Or a mixture? How students perceive us is important. They need someone they are comfortable with and can learn from. Teachers knowing how students feel about them can help in developing and maintaining supportive relationships. Feedback from a survey provides insight on what improvements are needed to strengthen or begin bonds and improve the learning environment. If you are serious about improving or maintaining your relationship with students, take a moment out of class to ask students to write three to five adjectives or sentences that describe you. This is preferably for lower-grade level students. Make sure to stress no physical attributes, just personality and characteristically. For younger students, you may want to post a word bank for them to pull from. Encourage students to be honest and allow them to remain anonymous to not interfere with the reliability of the survey. They are more likely to be authentic in providing you an insight on how they perceive you. Additionally, clearly explain the purpose of the data you will collect. It is to help *you* improve as their teacher. The survey is pointless if the feedback is not utilized to enhance your relationship with them. Use the charts (Figures 3 and 4) at the end of the chapter to think about your current practices and ways to improve them. Please note: On a wider range, many districts give formal surveys to individual students that focus on teacher relationships and effectiveness. Inquire from administration to access this feedback.

Around my seventh year of teaching, I was once called into my principal's office to have my annual mid-year conference. It was a time to formatively assess the productivity of my learning environment, teaching practices, and instructional decisions, and to evaluate the overall academic progress of my effectiveness. As I sat in my principal's office, I began to reflect on the school year with him. He was a matter-of-fact, direct type of leader who was relatively new with two years in as principal. He was one who didn't sugarcoat anything, and although he was a tough cookie to work with, I learned a lot under his leadership. I expressed my concern to him about the challenges with some students on my team. Student behaviors were negatively impacting the learning environment for students, and the teachers were fed up. As the department chairperson, I represented my and the department's concerns. There were students who had been suspended several times already both in school and out of school, and it was only mid-semester; there was little to no parental involvement, and the parents who were involved had little impact on changing their child's behavior; parents would be contacted about their child's negative behaviors; some would promise things would improve, but little change was made. Students seemed not to care about the consequences of their behavior, so we were basically left on our own to create our own effective discipline management plan in an attempt to remedy the problems.

My principal responded to my comments and stated, "I hear your concern, but…"

"But?" I thought. "there isn't a but." I continued to listen as he talked.

"You all teach the same students, correct?"

"Yes," I replied.

He went on, "So why is it that the same students who act out in your colleagues' classes are the same students who do their work and are engaged in your class?" he stated, in a mater-of-fact way.

He continued on to say that he and other administration never observed those same types of behaviors in my class that I spoke of. He followed with examples, then focused on one specifically. Unruly students were usually placed in my class, despite their grade level or the subject they were in at the time. He continued saying that, "Every time administration comes to retrieve the students from your class, the children say the same thing, 'I want her to be my teacher.'"

I went silent with no rebuttal to possibly slip from my tongue; he was right. I began to reflect before answering. Still trying to defend my team members, I responded, "We all have different personalities; just like a child may deal with their father differently than their mother; we can't expect teachers to be the same." Although possibly true, my justification wasn't accepted and my response was quickly negated. Instead, he charged me with the task of engaging in deep, risky conversations with my team members about their student-teacher relationship practices and to develop and share my methods that were working for me and ways in which my department could benefit from them.

As I left his office, wheels were turning in my head, and I never took the time to realize this truth. Why were students respecting my authority and not some of my coworkers? What was I doing in my classroom that they weren't? Why did the *bad* kids want to be in my class? We taught the same students, but why would students perform better academically and behaviorally in my class than in others? Was it because I taught a subject students liked more than the others? Was it because they saw me as young and hip? Everyday, we would share stories, or rather gossip, about students and what crazy things they had said or done in class that day. I would have stories to tell but was usually shocked to hear the outrageous incidents of how students were acting in my colleagues' classes, since I had never seen that side of them. In other cases, I knew a different side existed, but never had to personally experience it. Now, I'm not saying they were angels for me all the time, let's be clear, but the extent to how the kids were with other teachers was not that extreme for me.

The talk with my teammates occurred, but no matter the ideas suggested or developed—even the ones that were tried but were not successful—when I reevaluated the plan, the root of the problems were the same across the board. The teachers with the most challenges had never built a meaningful relationship with their students—at all. They didn't know how, or looking back, maybe the bitterness towards students had already manifested and acted as a wall that prohibited any feelings to get through. Teachers had become so fed up with non-compliant students that they were mentally and physically done and went into a day-to-day mode of "just getting by" with students, which included ignoring them, making them stand in the hallway the entire class period while handing them their work with little or no expectation for it to be completed, and sitting them in the back of the class so they would become invisible and quiet. Because my teammates didn't implement the methods we discussed with fidelity, student behaviors never improved. Building relationships with my students came easier for me, for the most part. There were some difficult situations where it took an act of God to get them on my side, and even then it wasn't an all win-win situation. There were a few that I simply would rather not get to know, and in fact, I wish they transferred. But, despite the tough students, I was always able to get a breakthrough no matter how minor or major; students would walk away knowing I cared even if they took me through hell and back to realize it. A culmination of experiences is to blame for my method of building relationships. As a new teacher a few years in, I would observe the best teachers and their interactions with students. These teachers made students feel important and human. These teachers would sit at the cafeteria table with students even when they didn't have to and eat lunch with them. Students enjoyed it and hurried to get their lunch tray to sit near.

I observed other teachers having conversations with students about everyday life. These teachers were friendly and would laugh with students and smile at them and compliment them on even the smallest thing such as liking their shiny notebook. These teachers were so well connected with students that they knew about students' home life and would ask how mom or a brother was doing. They would show up at games and other extracurricular activities. These teachers loved their students but kept their academic expectations high. They expected students to do their best and wouldn't allow any slack. These teachers could chastise their students about any of their wrongdoing, and the students would receive it without reprimand; I sought to be like them. A culmination of teachers, including those in my family, molded me into the kind of teacher I wanted to become.

When I first entered the profession, I thought I had to leave my private life private and allow students to see me as a teacher only. But through my observations, I learned to become more personable. My undergrad studies taught me the psychology of child development, but as far as the how-to's in the inner city, I was left fending on my own; fortunately, I learned.

Don't allow relationships to be salvaged beyond your desire to repair it. Therefore, understand the value of having good relationships with students. It will make the classroom environment more controllable, and let's be real, we have to be able to control our classrooms in order for teaching and learning to occur. The pressure of teacher accountability speaks for itself; if there is no proven record of student progress, all fingers will point towards you; you will go on record as an ineffective teacher, which leaves an unwanted paper trail that becomes your reputation, and most importantly, we are forming our future architects, doctors, technicians, lawyers, entrepreneurs, artists, and musicians; our children need us just as much as we need them. From day one, get to know your students' interests.

Include a purposeful questionnaire similar to the one in Figure 2 to gain an understanding of students' activities and interests, family life, and goals; the example can be adopted and adapted to provide the most useful information to better fit your course subject and grade level. You won't remember every student's response; however, attempt to, by keeping the form readily available by placing the questionnaires in a file for your review as the year progresses. It will be informative to glimpse back at them as needed. The data collected from the questionnaire can be used in various ways. Students will have a chance to think about themselves and become aware of who they are and what they need from you. Listen to them. Additionally, the information can be implemented into the curriculum. You will be able to plan differentiated lessons and activities based on their interests and needs. For example, through this questionnaire, you may learn that a student prefers working individually versus in a group setting, since he or she usually falls off course when working with peers. Or, you may discover that a student does not have internet access at home and may be able to assign alternative work or find technology resources to aid the student at home.

Supporting Your Students' Emotional Needs

Taking time to support your students emotionally is imperative to helping them academically. Attending to your students' needs doesn't magically happen; it is an investment that requires intentional processes that are developed as we do our everyday work. How you build the culture of your classroom is ongoing and takes a true desire to connect with all learners in order to establish and maintain a positive relationship and improve student

Getting to Know Your Student Questionnaire

BASIC INFORMATION

Name

Name you would like to be called?

When is your birthday?

Are you new to this school?

Where were you before?

Any siblings that attend the school now or previously?

Do you have internet access at home?

Who are your close friends in this class?

INTERESTS AND ACTIVITIES

What are your hobbies?

Have you been involved (or are you hoping to become involved) in any school activities (clubs, sports, etc.)? If so, which ones?

What is something you do well?

Name three words to describe yourself.

What are things that bother you? (gets on your last nerve)

My favorite snacks are:

LEARNING AND GOALS

I learn the most when the teacher...

I work better in groups? Alone? With a partner? With the teacher?

Because......

I don't like it when teachers...

What are your educational goals after high school?

My ideal job would be...

If you have a job, how many hours per week do you work?

What do you see yourself doing in the next 5-10 years?

How do you plan to get to where you want to be 5-10 years from now?

Figure 2– Created by Christina Edwards (2016)

achievement. Maslow's hierarchy of needs states that once our physiological needs are met, then our emotional needs become most important. Think about a time you sat in a faculty meeting and dreaded being there. You may not remember what the topic of discussion was; you may not have participated or asked questions; however, I am sure you can recall vividly how you felt being there. Now think about how your students may feel in class. Evidence on how our brains function suggests that emotion is significantly intertwined in the learning process (Weiss, 2000). There are developmental and emotional changes students experience, and at times, learning is last on a student's agenda. However, teachers *need* for students to learn! This poses a major conflict between teachers and their students. While younger students desire approval from adults, students in latter grades are fighting for power and interdependence from adults. Therefore, how can we support students in our class, even when they may not desire to be there? This can be obtained by understanding their emotions. We may see a student acting out, but what we don't see are their feelings. What is the cause of the undesired behavior? How do we address it so that the child's emotional needs are met? The truth is, even as an adult, if I felt my school leaders undervalued me as an employee, or they only focused on work, or they didn't recognize my achievements, but rather criticized my work, I wouldn't want to be there. I would shut down and seek other employment. Students need to feel that they belong; they need to feel significance, they need power; they need to feel that you genuinely care. When these needs are not met, they become frustrated and exhibit what we label as misbehavior. Building your class culture is imperative before any learning can take place. Students should feel safe, nurtured, empowered, and that they matter. Make taking care of their emotional needs a priority, and understand it is ongoing.

Quick Note: Teaching New Generations

In order to meet the emotional needs of students, you must first understand who they are in today's world. Your current students are in the world of technology and social media, and future generations of students will become even more advanced and tech-savvy. These students will never know life without technology, with cursive writing, or life with home phones. The once-used card catalogs in the media center to search for library books are now replaced with computerized ways to locate books. Home phones are replaced with smartphones, where any information can be retrieved by talking to a smartphone or computer. Technology is used to soothe irritated children—and their parents. The best way students contact each other is through snapping pictures and videos and posting them online, and communicating via text messaging or through posts. Herbert Simon, an economist and psychologist stated, "A wealth of information creates a poverty of attention." Attention is the psychological tool we use to tune out irrelevant information so we can focus on what is important to us. As the information available to us expands exponentially, our attention is increasingly strained and challenged. "Our students focus on what's relevant to them. Teachers are in an uphill battle to give students the information they need to know in order to be successful, but it is not always received smoothly if it is viewed as irrelevant.

We are certainly in a different day in time. Students in this generation have mastered multitasking and have a very short attention span. They want only the information they need. They want options; they want to understand why; they want to feel included. Everything needs to be instant, or you can just forget about it. How does this impact our classrooms? How is this generation influencing the way we are teaching? As we are building relationships with students, we must consider how to better connect. Tim Elmore, founder of Growing Leaders, provides a deepened understanding into the world of Centennials, also known as Generation Z. He gives four simple ways to give students what they need.

1. **Shift from playing the "hero" to playing the "guide" or supportive role.** "People become engaged when they are the hero of the story. This means your role shifts from supervisor to consultant. You're not a sage on the stage, but a guide on the side."
2. **Support the issues that are at the core of what matters most to teens today.** "Instead of always demanding students to 'get on board' with your subject and your ideas, what if you enabled them to choose what matters to them (within the confines of your class or topic) and you help them pursue it?"
3. **Utilize various social media platforms to enable them to curate themselves.** "Most teens are still figuring out who they are. The best way adults can help them is through guiding their involvement with real—not virtual—experiences."

Responsive Teaching Teaching in the 21st century demands that all teachers are culturally proficient to effectively service their students. Teachers must do this by utilizing culturally responsive teaching practices in order to connect with learners. Zaretta Hammond, teacher and author of Culturally Responsive Teaching and the Brain, provides a deepened understanding of the mindset teachers must have in order to accelerate learners while reaching the goal of equity, or giving *each* student the necessary resources they need in order to thrive. (interview)

> "The promise of cultural responsive teaching is being able to bridge learning gaps students have and meeting [those] standards. Testing alone is not going to

change anything in terms of what students know and are able to do, But when we actually learn how to maximize the cultural tools they already bring for learning to the classroom, we overlook them; we don't take advantage of them. When we understand what they are and we're able to capitalize off of that, we are going to see an acceleration in students' ability to move the needle on their own learning."

Many teachers who enter inner city schools lack the background and training to grasp their students' social and emotional needs, while others are too outdated with current times. They have zero understanding of the diverse population of students they serve; therefore, they cannot initially connect with students personally, which interferes with students academically. Teachers must go beyond the school's four walls to connect with students. Weinstein, Tomlinson-Clark, and Curran (2004) explain that "by bringing our implicit, unexamined cultural biases to a conscious level, we are less likely to misinterpret the behaviors of our culturally different students and treat them equitably." Being culturally aware is constant. As years progress, your awareness of the cultural needs of the students you teach may need retouching. Refresh yourself each school year, since times quickly change. One group of students may be totally different from the next group of students. To do this, sign up for workshops and training, whether offered locally or nationally. Although many school districts may not provide funding to cover workshop expenses, attending on your own will be a great investment. Additionally, focus on gathering support from educators like you. Teachers, counselors, staff developers, and administrators who work together to build community have a better chance to improve their practice than educators who work independently and in isolation (Lindsey & Lindsey D.B., Martinez 2007).

There has been a well-hypothesized widening cultural mismatch between teachers and the students they teach. This shift has arrived. Reportedly, white, middle aged women account for the majority of school teachers; however, there is an increase of students of color. According to the National Education Association (2014), projections to the year 2021 indicate higher public school enrollments for African Americans, Hispanics, Asian/Pacific Islanders, Native Americans/Alaska Natives, and students of two or more races, and lower enrollments for whites. For the first time in history, children of color will dominate grades K-12. Although the racial and ethnic makeup of the country's school systems are shifting, the racial and ethnic backgrounds of teachers will not be as diverse. White female teachers dominate and will continue to dominate the profession. White teachers have to build a solid relationship with their minority students because their students may respond differently to teachers who don't look like them. To be a successful white teacher in a non-white classroom, white teachers must recognize students' non-dominant culture and learn how to engage with it pedagogically (Gay & Howard, 2000; Ladson-Billings, 2009; Milner, 2011). There are stereotypes and assumptions that are adopted through personal life's experiences. Keep them out the classroom. It hinders relationships and interconnectedness with students. The assumptions, values, and beliefs that educators hold about students and their parents are manifested in our actions, interactions, and non-actions (Lindsey & Lindsey D., B., Martinez 2007). Non-minority teachers, just like minority teachers, adapt well and flourish when they make connections with their students. Their success is attributed to their understanding of the children in the students' own environment. If you are a non-minority teacher, understand your identity as a white American. You may not have come from a privileged family, or maybe so. However, some students will look at you as dominating, regardless. They hear conversations and witness and experience racial inequalities and injustices; they watch disturbing law-enforcement practices on television and on social media; they have experiences that may be unlike yours if you don't look like them. Always strive to be fair and never tolerate disrespect from students no matter the opposition, so establish and enforce your expectations. Some students will challenge you while others will be bystanders/onlookers. Others will accept you without issue. When students get used to you and realize you are genuinely there for them, they are more likely to respect your authority; however, it can be an uphill battle; it takes time to develop. Learn and implement students' community into lessons. They are prone to be more engaged when the lesson is relevant to their background. Most importantly, always hold all students to a high academic standard; anything less should be intolerable. Students need caring, effective teachers who are willing to go the extra mile for all students in their care, regardless of race, ethnicity, and background. Understand that this does not mean minority teachers automatically are accepted and respected by students; in the same way, building a welcoming foundation with students is necessary.

Regardless of race, students need genuine teachers who really care. Students may see you as different, but celebrate—don't tolerate—all differences. I can't reiterate this point enough. You are not here to rescue "these children" from their environment, because if that is the attitude, you've already lost. Understand your role is to work with the community to ensure each child's success.

How do we prepare current and future educators for the cultural change? The best way to address this gap and be an effective teacher is to be culturally aware of yourself, the environment in which you teach, and the diverse population of students in which you teach. This approach is rooted in culturally responsive pedagogy (Gay 2000), which means learning about students' backgrounds, families, and communities, so that we ground our curricula and instruction with their experiences and interests. Some of the characteristics of culturally responsive teaching are:

1. **Positive perspectives on parents and families:** Teachers should engage in dialogue with parents as early as possible about parents' hopes and aspirations for their child, their sense of what the child needs, and suggestions about ways teachers can help.
2. **Communication of high expectations:** All students should receive the consistent message that they are expected to attain high standards in their school work.
3. **Learning within the context of culture:** Gain knowledge of the cultures represented in their classrooms and adapt lessons so that they reflect ways of communicating and learning that are familiar to the students.
4. **Student-centered instruction:** Learning is cooperative, collaborative, and community-oriented.
5. **Culturally mediated instruction:** Instruction and learning take place in an environment that encourages multicultural viewpoints and allows for inclusion of knowledge that is relevant to the students.
6. **Reshaping the curriculum:** The curriculum should be integrated, interdisciplinary, meaningful, and student-centered.
7. **Teacher as facilitator:** Teachers should develop a learning environment that is relevant to and reflective of their students' social, cultural, and linguistic experiences.

(Ladson-Billings, 1994).

In order to be successful teaching diverse learners, one must reflect on his or her own values, beliefs, and behaviors. Are we focused on teaching the kids we currently teach or the kids we wish we were teaching? The goal is for teachers to be successful teaching any population of students. Attend professional workshops and training from the district and beyond that targets cultural awareness and proficiency. Partner with an experienced teacher who has been in your shoes and is excelling. Build a bridge to embrace student and teacher differences and be sensitive to all cultures. Don't expect students to integrate into your world, but rather immense yourself into theirs in order to reach them personally and cognitively. Inner city students are not middle- or upper-class children; their experiences are much different from their counterparts. Let's be clear, culture does not only equate to race. It is the social habits, ethnicity, social class, family life, and sexual orientation, the shared patterns of behavior of a community of people. In order to effectively teach in this sector, there is a culture that must be acknowledged but not necessarily understood. There were many "codes of conduct" that students lived by that I could never grasp even though I often took interest in attempting to. Instead of being stand-offish, I acknowledged their world. On school spirit days, I would have on the latest, stylish sneakers. Students would be intrigued that a teacher wore trendy shoes that they considered "cool." Unbeknownst at that time, something as simple as shoes made a connection. It is true that fashion in the inner city makes a statement and earns status. My students could recognize the latest fashion trends better than I could. I would even sometimes speak students' jargon and sometimes not purposely. For example, as I was showing a video in class to reiterate a point of the lesson, I stated that some of the person's ideas were a little lame and stated my reasonings. As I continued to talk, their was a burst of laughter that became contagious throughout the class. I was confused as to what was so funny. One student made clear that I had used the word "lame" which was "their" language as another attempted to explain that I was trying to sound cool. But did students not understand how old that word was and how many times I've used that word in life, even when I was their age. Although I thought nothing major of the word, they thought it was everything, and in that moment, I got another "stripe" for being a cool teacher. Also, one advantage was that it wasn't hard for me to integrate my world into theirs since I am what I call an avid code switcher, being able to adjust to different environments, whether formally or informally. Be natural, don't try so hard. Students can distinguish the two.

Sneakers or (unintentional) slang may not be your thing, but there are ways to connect with students. You may have similar interests such as a favorite sports team or favorite dish, or you may take an interest in what they like, even if totally opposite of you. Either way, you have to get to know your students through conversation.

Additionally, students in this sector understand the cliché, "making a dollar out of fifteen cents" better than those of the privileged. No silver spoon was handed to them. Many of my students faced issues at home that adults, even myself, would have no idea how to handle. Some students would come to school to eat breakfast and lunch, and it may have been the only time they would eat for the day. Some would wash up in the restroom when no one was around, since there was no running water at home. Some received more attention from their teachers, whether positive or negative, than they received from home. Others slept in class or had an extensive poor attendance record because they were caring for their younger siblings late at night so their parent could work. Then there were others who had a strong foundation and support system and were expected to be and do their best, but circumstances have dictated for them to live according to their means. Understand your students' differences.

For example, my former colleague, a new special education teacher, traveled from an affluent area in California to an open position at my school for a teaching position. She had entered into a teacher education program and was required to teach in an inner city school for a couple of years to fulfill her program obligation. She was not fully aware of the treat she was in for. From day one, she was in total culture shock. Milner (2010) states, "cultural conflicts can cause inconsistencies and incongruence between teachers and students, which can make teaching and learning difficult" (p. 14). The students were aliens to her; she was totally disconnected from them. Her students gave her pure hell. She would try a plethora of strategies to focus on discipline and positive reinforcement, but nothing seemed to work. Unfortunately, she tried bribing them with candy and snacks, and that became their expectation. She relinquished her control when the students saw her crying on more than one occasion. One would think students would feel compassion and ease up from then on; however, this, like many other situations, was not the case. Unfortunately, students did not listen to her. They continued to act out, talk back, and disregard her authority. She would resort to getting other teachers to help control her class, which made her look weak to her students, and they were happy to call her out on it. They would even encourage her to go and get whomever she wanted to help. Although she would write disciplinary slips to administration, she felt unsupported by them. She expected students to be removed from class and suspended, whether it was an in-school or out-of-school suspension. This did not happen as often as she would have liked. Honestly, her issues stemmed from poor classroom management with the root issue of not understanding the community. She only had a perception of these students and did not educate herself prior to her hire and arrival. Although she was the lead teacher of a few class periods, she was my inclusion teacher, a special education teacher who works alongside a general education teacher to help meet special students needs. We shared a class for one period daily. I strived to model strategies for her that were researched-based and had worked for me both academically and behaviorally. I and a few others would share suggestions, and we would converse about methods that may have been useful to her particular group of students. She always stated that she tried everything. Unfortunately, her non-attempt to implement the strategies we discussed became evident the day I decided to take a restroom break as students worked. Before exiting our class, I asked her if she would be OK while I stepped out for a minute. Since the students were working diligently, there was no possible way there could be any problems. It was a huge error thinking she had everything totally under control, the biggest mistake ever. My class, who was working quietly, was now ironically, chaotic! I heard so much noise and disregard for her requests to "just shut up." As I walked down the hall. I questioned if it was my class, because I just left them doing their work. It couldn't be. I couldn't understand for the life of me what went wrong. However, I sympathized with her, giving my apology for that traumatic experience and chastised students for their misbehavior. To make a long story short, her situation never improved. She had had enough. She resigned after the first semester. I learned of it when I witnessed her enter the building early in the morning with assistance to remove her belongings piece by piece. I really felt bad for her and for her students. In a perfect world, the goal is for students to behave regardless if the teacher of record was in the room or not, even with a substitute; however, if students respect you enough, they will at least behave correctly in your presence. I reflected after she resigned. What was it that she did wrong? Did she even do anything wrong? Yes. She never took the time to connect with the students. She never entered into their world. If she did, maybe she wouldn't have taken the breakfast trays from students as they were eating in an attempt to rush them to their first period class, because they were probably genuinely hungry, or maybe she would have not only used generic classroom management strategies that never fit her population of students, or maybe instead of yelling at students, she could have just talked to them.

Research shows far too many educators, regardless of background, struggle to comprehend and employ the tenets of culturally responsive practice (NEA, 2014). Students would often say things like, "she doesn't like us, anyway." Although I never got that vibe from her, just as we should spend time understanding our students, students need time to understand us as well, but we have to create opportunities for practice in order for connections to occur. I'm positive that if she had taken the advice of myself and colleagues on how to establish relationships with her students, then things would have ended more positively, and she would have been able to handle her classes better, but she had already washed her hands of these students. However, as Noddings suggests, "No matter how hard educators try to care, if the caring is not received by students, the claim 'they don't care' has some validity" (2005, p. 15). Students shut down when they feel disconnected and distrust. Establish activities early to build community. According to Ellerbrock, Abbas, DiCicco, Denmon, Sabella, and Hart (2015), fostering a caring classroom community begins on the first day of school and continues throughout the school year. A caring educator:

- Establishes a safe and academic-focused classroom culture;
- Creates shared norms and values;
- Promotes open and honest communication;
- Makes time for everyone to get to know one another;
- Facilitates mutual respect;
- Encourages reciprocal care and mutual responsibility;
- Demands academic excellence from each student; and
- Uses student-centered cooperative group structures.

Build a welcoming environment for all students by getting to know them and facilitate the platform for students to learn about each other even during instruction. Allow discussions between students and yourself that demonstrate respect among differences. Don't leave your biases and assumptions at the door, erase them. Refrain from allowing racial or ethnic stereotypes to interfere with the way you perceive students. For example, Asian American students are stereotyped as achievers and hard workers, but what happens when your preconceived notion is incorrect with an Asian student who has entered your classroom? What if the student is in fact opposite of that achiever you knew they would be? How will you change your expectations? In a similar way, don't assume your students will understand American traditions such as cultural folklore. For example, a former colleague was teaching her lesson and made reference to an American folktale story. She assumed all her students knew the tale, but was sadly mistaken when the point she was trying to make was not received by the majority of her students. During her lesson, she had to quickly improvise so students could understand the point she was trying to make.

Furthermore, be mindful of students' socioeconomic status (SES). Many of us have no clue what life is like growing up in the communities where we teach. They are disadvantaged; that's no secret. The school systems in low-SES communities are often under-resourced, negatively affecting students' academic progress (Aikens & Barbarin, 2008). There are proven disparities between low-income families and those of middle and high class status; they are more at risk to fail. Research indicates that children from low-SES households and communities develop academic skills more slowly compared to children from higher SES groups (Morgan, Farkas, Hillemeier, & Maczuga, 2009). Students face overwhelming challenges, including forming social relationships with "outsiders," or those who are not from their neighborhood.

Establishing secure relationships with students is key. Students may be viewed as disrespectful, less empathetic to others, or having lack of manners, but one must first understand the deficits and then set clear expectation. If teachers are unfamiliar with student backgrounds, frustration will set in because we usually assume that students know how to act. The most important aspect is how you respond to students. Do we label the students as bad and just another product of their environment? Do we resort to engaging in ignominious behavior with them such as embarrassing them or calling out their behavior in front of their peers? Or, should we make provisions to lower the expectations for these students? No! We strive to change the behavior into a more desired one by setting norms through practice, demonstration, and application. A child's socioeconomic class is never the determining factor of their success. It certainly is no justification for limited success. School districts everywhere are aware of gaps in achievement in poverty-stricken communities; focus on strategies that address closing the gap and allow this bridge of action to counter the disparities.

Get In Where You Fit In

I once mentored a middle school teacher intern who couldn't catch a break. When teaching, he was dry, monotone in his speaking and his humor went over everyone's head. He didn't have any spark to his personality and voice. Even when he tried to make a joke, the students never understood his sense of humor. To be honest, if I was a student, I may have reacted to him the same way. No matter how much I spoke to him about adding "spunk" to his lessons or his voice, he wouldn't or probably didn't know how. Students didn't take to him well; they would try to pay attention but were bored out of their minds. I was his mentor teacher, so I felt responsible; I would model the expectation, but somehow, he would always fall short in his delivery, although there was slight improvement by the end of the semester. I was skeptical as if teaching was what he really wanted to do. During his second semester, as part of his program's requirement, he interned at a nearby high school and found his niche! He blossomed! Middle school was simply not his forte; high schoolers better suited his personality, and he really lit up when working with students. Know where you are better suited. It is hard to build a relationship with students when you aren't that into them. I was never interested in being an elementary teacher. No, I don't want to give hugs every two seconds. No, I don't want you to ask me for a bandaid for the cut you can barely see with the human eye. No, I don't want to put the cutesy decorations all over my classroom. I wasn't interested in that grade level. However, I knew where I was better suited. Several factors, such as energy level and personal and professional goals can help when evaluating what grade level you want to teach; each grade level range has its distinctive structures. When you are in your element, you are more likely to excel. Figure out where you fit and accelerate! You can't buy a personality, but understand as a teacher, you must have spontaneity in all grade levels; loosen up your energy level! Decide the subject you're most passionate about, and make sure it aligns with your personal goals. To determine where you may be a better fit, ask yourself these simple questions:

For elementary school,

1. Do I want to teach several subjects every day?
2. Do I want to see the same kids all day?
3. Am I interested in working with very young children and new learners?

4. Do I mind helping students tie their shoes or placing bandaids on a simple cut?
5. Am I creative and do I enjoy being crafty?

For middle school,

1. Am I OK with focusing on a single, specialized subject, or two?
2. Do I want to teach several sets of students on a daily basis?
3. Can I deal with students during the adolescent phase/puberty?
4. Do I want to sponsor a club or extracurricular activity? Ex: coaching a sport.

For high school,

1. Do I want to teach several specialized subjects? ex: Advanced placement courses.
2. Do I want to teach more than one grade level?
3. Am I OK with teaching young adults, 14-18 year olds?
4. Do I want to be an athletic coach as well?

Additionally, consider substituting to help find your niche. Or, during your field experience, see if your school allows you to student teach in more than one grade level band (grades K-5; 6-8; 9-12).

Respect is Reciprocal, Sometimes

When I was younger, I had a teacher who I was convinced did not like me. It was true, I was sure of it. I complained to my mother, a teacher. I was ready for her to confront the teacher about my

(HOW TO REALLY) BUILD STRONG TEACHER-STUDENT RELATIONSHIPS

allegations. My mother's response shocked me, "Your teacher is not there to like you. As long as she treats you fair, I'm good with that." "Well I'll be damned," I thought. But isn't that part of the job description? Shouldn't we as teachers like the students we teach? Not necessarily. No matter if my teacher did not like me, I was expected to still do her work and behave in class. Back then, that may have sufficed, but today's child will tune you completely out and cause havoc if they feel as if you don't like them. As a result, the struggles of teaching them becomes evident! One bad apple can definitely spoil a bunch. So, we have to approach this a different way. How do you take control of this? As a teacher, there were kids I simply did not like. Truth be told, I despised seeing them walking down the hall, and I dreaded the class period they were in; however, fake it until you make it! My artificial smile and greeting worked only because my actions emulated my smile and tone. Although I initially felt a negative way about them, I realized that some students weren't so bad after all. (I said some.) You will have to do that sometimes to make YOUR life easier. You have to stay sane. Meeting fire with fire will only cause catastrophe on YOU. You may not say anything negative to them, but your actions speak. Watch how you treat students. Some adults can be unethical and will use the little authority they have over students. Some even threatened students with failing grades, but it fell on deaf ears and fueled the fire even more. We can justify our negative actions all day long, and some will, but that justification won't change students' behavior into a more appropriate one. Only light can drive out darkness. Put on a happy face and do what you are charged to do, regardless. Find that child's interest. Engage in non-educational conversations. Laugh a little. Maybe, just maybe, you'll find out that that child wasn't so bad after all. Understand that this is not a one-size-fits-all strategy. You will experience times when you will give all the respect in the world, but it won't be reciprocated. Don't take it personally. Find that one positive attribute and focus on that. However, other situations need tough love. For example, during around my sixth year of teaching, one of my seventh grade students gave me so many problems. He was confrontational and so disruptive that I had to exclude him from the learning environment until he was ready to learn and ready to respect my classroom rules and procedures. I had to change the course. I had had enough. During dismissal, I pulled him to the side and calmly but directly told him that I really wanted to teach him and saw so much potential in him, but until he was ready and willing to learn, he would now have a seat away from students. I told him from that day forward, he could sit in the back of the class and quietly do whatever he wanted. This student now became invisible to me. I directed him back into the now-empty class and showed him where his new seat was. I told him that he was not allowed to raise his hands, talk to me or anyone. I expressed my dissatisfaction of how he constantly disturbed my classroom everyday. I spoke to him without raising my voice but I looked him dead in his eyes, did not blink or crack a smile, unthreatening. I made my appeal that I was always fair and respectful to him and that his disrespect to me in my classroom was unfair to me and all the learners. I then expressed how much I wanted him to be successful not only in my class, but in life, and I cared so much for his success. So I told him that when he starts to care, I will too, but until then, he was directed to sit in the back of the classroom every day. Go to sleep. Draw. Do whatever. But disturbing my class was not an option. I was not going to compromise the learning environment for others because he wanted to act a fool any longer. I was fed up! Students were not aware of our new arrangement. If I had made a scene in front of the class or even a small group, I'm sure he would have really been combative towards me. The next day, he entered the class and attempted to sit in his regular seat. We ended up catching eyes, and I nudged my head to his newly-assigned seat. He rolled his eyes, but went to his seat and he stayed in the seat. The first two days, he laid his head down and slept. Did this just backfire on me? Did I just give him exactly what he wanted? Although I wanted to go to his desk, shake him, yell at him, and make him do his work, I knew I couldn't give him a slap on the wrist; he needed tough love. After a couple of days in isolation, he attempted to mingle with the other kids with no interest in joining the learning environment, and I went to him and firmly reminded him of what we discussed. I privately went to the students grouped at their desks and told them that they were to speak with members of their group and no one else. After about the fifth day, he desired to ease back into the learning environment; I allowed him, instructing him where to sit. As he transitioned, I began working with him one on one and realized the main problem, which he was quite embarrassed about. There were many learning deficits. He had poor fluency and his comprehension was subpar. I had discovered the root. He was avoiding doing the work because he couldn't. Students with challenging behaviors are more likely to have academic deficits in reading, math, and written language (Lane, Carter, Pierson, & Glaeser, 2006). His behavior was avoidance. While the precise nature of the relationship between academic deficits and problem behavior remains unclear, indeed presenting a chicken-or-the-egg conundrum, we do know with some certainly that each influences the other in a reciprocal way (Scott, Nelson, & Liaupsin, 2001). Although this was a cycle a few times afterwards, his respect for me became more evident with time. From then on, all I had to do was give a look for him to straighten up. He would ask if he could get additional help after school, which I certainly obliged. He became very fond of me and I of him. He was really just a kid trying to hide his true deficits. Even the next school year, he would always come to my class to ask if I could help him with his work; he couldn't stay out, and I would have to close my door on him at times to make him get to his other classes on time. He would always give my class advice, "Don't play with my teacher."

Of course, experts won't advise to use this method, but tough love worked. I was looking to win the war, not the battle. You may have to be proactive with administration as to why a child is sitting off doing nothing if an observation is to occur, and if I had to take on that challenge, I would have gladly defended by actions. I was not a teacher with many discipline issues, so if I had to resort to this extent, administration would have backed me. That is the type of relationship you should establish with your school leaders. (In Chapter 5, we will discuss how to maintain a support channel with administration.) Choose your battles wisely. Nip issues in the bud to take control of your learning environment. Respect should be reciprocated, but it is not always. Be strategic when identifying ways to change the course of a misbehavior.

Maintain Self-Control

Unfortunately, some of our colleagues have lost their cool. You've seen them on Youtube and social media arguing and physically fighting—with students. It gets under my skin when another one bites the dust. So, I've stood in support of some of my colleagues without understanding the full circumstances. I've sympathized with them. Mainly because I know how buttons can be pushed. I've seen families of these students in the media in shock of how the teacher acted and not acknowledge their child's behavior or how the child cursed out a teacher like a sailor, or stood in their face in a threatening manner egging them on. "You are the professional/adult." "How do you talk to a child like that?" However, many who make these statements have no clue how it can go down. I have had similar situations where I've wanted to

(HOW TO REALLY) BUILD STRONG TEACHER-STUDENT RELATIONSHIPS

sweep the floor with students. It's true! I am one who is patient, slow to anger, fair, will take flight versus fight in any situation, but I've had my share of times when I've had to really snap back to reality, or I could have ended up on the news, too. So yes, I sympathize with those who couldn't walk away. The best thing to do is to never let it get to this point. In all of these situations, there were smaller incidences that escalated and got out of hand. Now, teachers who have a degree will lose their teaching certificate and have to search for other professions of work. Students will probably end up in an alternate school with a bright future still ahead of them. Losing self-control is embarrassing, and it's simply not worth your livelihood. Remember, you have everything to lose, and a student has nothing to lose. In modern times of social media and video cameras, watch your actions and words. Your uncontrollable behavior will be caught on video forever, even after you're gone. It's not worth it.

I've had to diffuse many student-teacher confrontations. I've also had students approach me to express how bad a teacher made them feel. Because of this, I've always been careful to avoid using unkind, unnecessary words and sarcasm with students. Kids, like adults, can be ruthless with words. You can only control your tongue and how you react to disrespect. In one particular case, for example, students would talk bad about the teacher, and it hurt her feelings, although she played tough. Unfortunately, she would engage in "jonning" (talking negatively towards each other) matches with students which she thought was helping to enforce her power, but arguing with a child does nothing to improve your relationship with them; it actually weakens your authority. In the cafeteria one day, a student had gotten so angry with her that the student yelled out a very rude comment to her. The cafeteria, filled with students, started laughing unanimously. She responded with, "Your mama!" This caused a major disruption in the entire cafeteria. Teachers' lunch time was now disturbed and they had to rush to calm down students from their excitement of what had just taken place. Other staff members who were in the cafeteria were totally caught off guard as to what had just taken place and had to help diffuse the situation. The student was wired up and embarrassed and seemed ready to physically attack the teacher. It took a a few staff members to escort the student out of the cafeteria. Needless to say, an administrator witnessed it all and the teacher was called into the office later that day. This situation could have been avoided by not allowing it to get that far. Maintain control of your tongue at all times. It is so easy to transform to disrespectful behavior, but don't! In fact, it makes it tougher to build respect with not only the student, but with your other students. Although, not impossible. For your sanity, put on a front, and for heaven's sake, don't let them see you sweat. That front may end up breaking barriers, so release the grudges and start every day fresh. Although the situation was bad, it could have been so much worse. No matter how much kids will push your buttons, don't allow yourself to lose it. In the words of Michelle Obama, "when they go low, we go high."

Avoid Power Struggles

It happens time and time again. Understand this, you won't win. Focus on the bigger picture. Keep your composure and take control of your emotions; don't take it personally. I've witnessed students getting a rise out of teachers, and the only place a teacher can go after this is downhill. You don't want to be one of the ones going to tribunal—a school board hearing where serious disciplinary action is rendered—when a teacher (or student) is believed to have violated the code of conduct, to save your job for saying something unprofessional and inappropriate, because you've allowed a student to make you go there. Don't lose your power by arguing; students will test your limitations to see how far you will go. I would never allow students to see my limit because, honestly, teachers are limited to what we can do. You set your own fear level. Don't allow students to be disrespectful, but know how to curtail that undesired behavior. There can only be one chief and that's YOU. If you have to discipline a student, and you will, choose which battle you will get tough in. Be firm, nip the problem in the bud, and transition to another subject. Don't well on it. Don't feed it too much attention. Address it, then continue business as usual. Have a short-term response and adopt cool-off methods such as pausing and thinking before finding the best time to speak again. Also, silence is golden; sometimes that is the best thing to do. Count to ten before responding. As for my favorite method, I had to talk to God. "Help me Lord" is all I could sometimes say under my breath. Students were well aware of the moment(s) I needed, and looking back, it's funny how they would encourage their peers to "leave her alone right now." You can only go so far, so disburse your authority wisely. Not every battle has to be won.

Show Interest In What Students Care About

Nothing says how much you care more than showing up. It means everything to a student to see you show interest in them by attending and supporting them in an extracurricular event outside of normal school hours. I will admit I wasn't at every game, but the ones I did show up to, I was cheering and wishing them well. The next day, they would come up to me and thank me for being there. They were so happy. If possible, be a coach or a sponsor. I coached track and field, became a cheerleading and dance team sponsor, and coached the softball team. I had no experience in any, but that's beside the point. No one else took on the responsibility, so I did. I learned a lot from the team and it brought a sense of unity. There were many students who I did not teach or never taught, but when I would see those students with their friends, I took on another form to them. I wasn't only labeled a teacher in the school, but I became Coach. I met, had conversations, and laughed and joked with parents at games, which benefited me in the classroom and beyond. Being able to let my hair down in this informal setting established genuine connections. Parents knew I was involved and invested in their child. I was building relationships with the community; positive dialogue is captivating and builds trust. Plan to show up, whether it be to a student's church event, a recital, or family celebration.

Throughout my teaching years, I was invited by parents to some other functions such as baby showers, family gatherings, and church functions. Use your discretion before agreeing to attend any of these events. Although I would not mind attending any daytime extracurricular games, I did not want to get too personal and would politely turn down any invitations to such events. As a professional, there are boundaries that you must maintain. For example, I was invited to one of my student's parent's baby shower, but I politely declined. However, I sent a couple of ABC baby books instead by the student. Do not send anything too personal; keep it reasonably priced and simple. However, sending a gift is totally up to you.

On the contrary, I have attended a few funerals of a student's close family member. The setting is more public. Once again, use your discretion, and check with the district's handbook to make sure attending outside functions are not prohibited.

Show Up Even If Noone Else Does

Immerse yourself into their lives. You get a firsthand account of how students live and what the home front is like. I had a student who was a real headache. There was no home structure, and she really felt like an outcast. She had a sister who was also in the same grade, but you could clearly identify the family's favorite child. The two looked different, and I believe that may have been part of the problem. One was considered prettier than the other. My student loved basketball and would talk about every team in the NBA. Who lost, who won, the statistics. Everything. I knew that was her interest, and I began having conversations with her about it, and she would talk my head off. She told me what recreational team she played for and how she was the star of the team! She wanted so badly for me to come. The first two games, I couldn't make it. She would ask me, "You coming to my game?" So, one afternoon, I surprised her and showed up after work. That was the beginning of something beautiful; the game for me seemed like practice. There was no one there, and it just looked like kids running up and down the court throwing the ball aimlessly. The game lasted maybe 30 minutes, but me showing up was so special to her; it meant everything. She cherished that day, and from that day forward, I was the teacher other teachers would send her to when she was removed from class. (She even started doing things purposely so she could get out of class and sit in mine.) But when I reprimanded her, she would listen and comply. She secretly wanted the discipline; she desired the attention. Nobody at the home front provided the attention she sought or cared enough. When she wanted to talk, I was there. Did I never have to redirect her behavior in my class? Of course I did, but dealing with her was like night and day compared to my counterparts. I attended a few more games but, unfortunately, never was able to meet a parent. During one particular phone call I made, I understood what my student's home life was like. Nothing she did seemed right in the eyes of her parent. There was so much negativity that even when I was calling for something positive, the parent seemed to only focus on the negative. It was true, the student had a history of disciplinary issues that seemed to stain her mother's relationship with her. The home front wasn't the best. I get it, but this was still a child. Despite this, I know my student remembers even to this day that I really cared. I was happy to have shown up for her. Children will always be children, and many grow up too fast. When students see you take time out of your day to immerse in their lives, they will remember it. I often think about how she is now. These are the stories of the inner city that remind me of why our job is so important. All students possess positive characteristics; don't overlook and undervalue them. It is our job to hone in on those attributes to develop the whole child.

Teachers and Gender

There is a dearth of male teachers in our inner city public schools. Females, hands down, dominate the teaching profession, just as one may take notice of a dominance of females as nurses. According to the National Center for Education Statistics, in 2011-12, some 76 percent of public school teachers were female while 24 percent were male. How many male teachers did you have while a student, compared to female? More male teachers enter into our junior and high schools, but it is safe to say that we need a few good men in our classrooms to close this gender disparity in the teaching profession.

Many of my students came from single-parent homes. It was uncommon for a two-parent household, where a dependable male and female role model existed. I observed male students had greater opposition towards male authority figures within the school, and I often wondered why. I have witnessed male teachers having to resign for losing their cool in lieu of being sent to tribunal with a possibility of getting their teaching certificate revoked while protecting their female colleagues or defending themselves. Male students seemed to have a higher tolerance for female authority than male authority. It's important for male authority figures to take into consideration that there may not be a decent, dependable male around, so be strategic when disciplining. From experience, male students were used to showing opposition to their mother's significant other, usually not their biological dad. Any male chastising them, whether at school or at home, was highly unflavored, and students were blatantly defiant even to males in administrative roles. Cushman's (2008) study stated that schools need more male teachers to compensate for a lack of male presence in homes. In many schools, any interactions students have with males are those in administrative roles/principal, custodians, or coaches. In order for males to be successful, first understand that it may take time before male students warm up to you. The parent may warm up to male teachers more in hopes to give their child a role model, or someone their child can relate to. Pay attention to students' social-emotional needs. Discover if you share a common interest such as sports, music artists, a board game, or video game, and use it as leverage to build a relationship with students. Be consistent and fair to earn their respect and model the same characteristics that you desire for your students.

Same for female teachers; some mothers did not provide a stable home front. You be that example. Unfortunately, television and music don't provide a good demonstration to what a woman or man of integrity should reflect, especially for those of color. I've been a sucker for reality shows and music for entertainment purposes, but direct examples of what the true essence of a role model is, lacks. Most of my male students desired to be a rapper or athlete with no alternative in sight. Introduce that student who likes to draw to architecture, or set up that student who enjoys cooking to a trip with a local chef. Introduce that student who cleans up the room nicely to business ownership and entrepreneurship. It's never too early to introduce opportunities. Initiate career days. There are many careers that students aren't even aware of. Thank goodness students have you! Many students have not had the pleasure of visiting neighboring countries, states, or even other cities within their own state, so plan field trips. Begin an organization/club. Set the example. Raise funds because, unfortunately, there is a possibility the school's budget may be limited and unable to sponsor field trips.

Because my experiences of a male teacher were nonexistent in elementary, I was elated to have male teachers in junior high. It was different for me but enjoyable. I still appreciated my female teachers but anticipated more male teachers in high school and beyond. In brief, great teachers can be male and female. No matter the teacher's gender, students should always have positive experiences.

Draw Your Own Conclusion

We often read reviews before seeing a movie, or we ask the waiter how a dish tastes before we order it, but how many times after you've received a negative report have you proceeded anyway and found it totally opposite of what you were told? We do this with students. We inquire about them from their previous teachers, or sometimes, the negative reports find us. Make up your own conclusion about a student. Don't allow fellow teachers to tell you about problem students beforehand. Form your own opinions based off your experiences. I often discovered that the students

I was usually warned about were nothing like their description. And, don't taint a relationship for the next teacher because of your own bad experiences with them. If there is something of extremity that may be very necessary to share, then refer the teacher to seek their personal records to investigate any documents that need to be known. But develop your own personal experiences with the child instead of allowing others to hypothesize your relationship with students. How a student is with one may not be how he or she is with you.

If you are not teaching our students for the right reasons, as one educator to another, leave the profession. You are doing more harm to the children than good. A teacher's influence goes way beyond the few months you have them in your room; it never ends. I bet you can remember who your favorite teachers were and can give specific examples of why they were your favorite. On the contrary, you can vividly describe your worst teachers and can give a dissertation-length speech about their negative attributes. Whether good or bad, students will remember you. Inner city kids need you. You may be the only shining light they see. I know some teachers who should have never signed up for this profession. They had a tough time in their career, those are the ones that I don't feel sorry for; the kids are the ones I have empathy for. They had to endure a teacher who didn't care, one who came to work already ready to leave and didn't give two cares whether they learned or not. Leave a good lasting impression. You are the supporter, their encouragement. Treasure your investment. Will you be the teacher students feel they can turn to, and will you be their advocate? What will students say about you in ten years? I often strive to be like my grandmother, Dr. Jacquelyn Ponder, a former teacher, director, and principal in the same district where I once worked. She retired in the early 90s, and I didn't start teaching until over ten years later; however, over twenty years after her retirement, former teachers, colleagues, students, and parents continue to celebrate her. They still hold recognition ceremonies to honor the lasting impression she has had and still has on them. This is the legacy I want to leave, we should all want to leave. What you say and do are being closely monitored by students. I never realized how even the polish on my fingernails would connect me with students. They see you when you don't even expect it. Be a great example for them, your position is an automatic role model. You must walk the walk and talk the talk. What do you want students to remember about you? How will your actions ensure that you achieve this goal?

Elementary Student Survey	Check one	
My teacher is kind to me.	☐ Yes ☐ No	☐ Sometimes ☐ I'm not sure
I have fun learning in this class.	☐ Yes ☐ No	☐ Sometimes ☐ I'm not sure
My teacher treats me with respect.	☐ Yes ☐ No	☐ Sometimes ☐ I'm not sure
My teacher always helps me when I need them to.	☐ Yes ☐ No	☐ Sometimes ☐ I'm not sure
My teacher listens to me.	☐ Yes ☐ No	☐ Sometimes ☐ I'm not sure

Figure 3

Student Survey	Check one	
In this class, I feel that my teacher cares about me.	☐ Always ☐ Never	☐ Sometimes
I feel that my teacher likes me.	☐ Always ☐ Never	☐ Sometimes
How excited are you about going to this class?	☐ Always ☐ Never	☐ Sometimes
In this class, my teacher is respectful towards me.	☐ Always ☐ Never	☐ Sometimes
My teacher appreciates when I join in on class discussions.	☐ Always ☐ Never	☐ Sometimes

Figure 4

Refection

I desire to be a teacher who...

Students perceive me as....

To build better relationships with my students, I ...

I can start today by....

My most memorable teacher was..........

he/she is remembered most because....

Therefore........

Figure 5

Classroom Management that Boosts Student Achievement

There may be no greater hurdle in public schools today than that presented by students who exhibit challenging behavior.
—WESTLING

ACCORDING TO DATA from the latest National Center for Education Statistics' Schools and Staffing Surveys, turnover rates are 50 percent higher for teachers in Title I schools, which serve more low-income students. Mathematics and science teacher turnover rates are nearly 70 percent greater in Title I schools than in non-Title I schools, and turnover rates for alternatively certified teachers are more than 80 percent higher.

Sure! We've seen layoffs in recent years; however some of the main reasons of the high turnover rate are due to the pressures of teacher accountability and burnout. The overall consumption of managing difficult classrooms makes working conditions dissatisfying. Inner city schools are the most difficult to retain teachers and fill those positions. According to McKinney (2005), urban teachers leave the profession within the first five years of their career, citing behavior problems and management as factors influencing their decision to leave. Something must be done and it must be done quickly! Research indicates that teachers' actions in their classrooms have twice as much impact on student achievement as assessment policies, community involvement, or staff collegiality; and a large part of teachers' actions involves the management of the classroom (Marzano, 2003; Marzano & Marzano, 2003). We've all entered the school's hallway and have heard pure chaos coming from a colleague's classes despite the door being closed. Students loud, teacher scrambling to get the class under control, absolutely no teaching and learning occurring, or maybe you have the classes that are usually "turned up" in this way. I've felt sorry for the teacher for lack of control because usually he or she is a ticking time bomb, and it's only a matter of time before an explosion happens among students or with the teacher him or herself. Some of us have never grown up in this type of school environment before and may be experiencing major problems with classroom management. What teacher wants to be angry all the time? What teacher wants to yell at students all day, every day? What teacher wants to go home feeling defeated and frustrated and take it out on their loved ones who are casualties of war, only to return the next day for a repeat? No one. We can continue to put the blame on these kids for being too aggressive or out of control. Besides, it's them, not you, right? Absolutely not. Unless there are factors out of your control, in no way should you not have control over your class.

Classroom management is not isolated to discipline problems; it is defined as an intentional set of practices that aid in maintaining a smooth and positive learning environment for all students. Classes should always stay organized and managed, and the learning environment should flow despite possible disruptions. Managing a class is not always simple; it can be a challenge. You don't begin teaching, and everyone suddenly quiets down because of their high interest level in the subject you teach. You don't request that everyone pay attention and it happens instantaneously because, in some cases, it doesn't happen at all. Sometimes it takes a loud voice, a whistle, a flicking of the lights, a demand. Even then, some students won't join the bandwagon at first and get quiet as desired. Unfortunately, I can't provide a secret magic trick to sprinkle over your classroom to make students behave as you wish. However, there are strategies and techniques that will limit distractions and encourage positive behavior among students in hopes that it becomes contagious to the masses. Authors such as Dr. Sean Yisreal has written literature such as The Cleopatra Teacher Rules and Classroom Management: A Guide for Urban School Teachers to provide strategies that will help teachers deal with the unique challenges faced in urban schools.

In Marzano and Marzano's (2003) meta-analysis of more than 100 studies, they found that teachers who had positive relationships with their students had 31 percent fewer disciplinary problems and rule violations over the course of the year than teachers who did not have positive relationships with their students. Managing difficult behavior is a serious problem among elementary, middle, and high school teachers of the inner city; most importantly, is interferes with the academic environment. Poor classroom management results in lost instructional time, feelings of inadequacy, and stress (Sayeski, Brown 2011). What you do on the first days of school matters; however, it does not determine how successful your school year will be. In fact, it is what you do between the first day of school and the last that matters most. Don't mind such cliches as, "You will either win or lose your class on the first days of school if you don't lay down the law," or "Don't smile for the first few weeks." Within a school year, I've witnessed the strictest teachers lose their power and the weakest teachers gain their strength. However, slow and steady wins the race. Why is it important to establish rules initially? How do you organize and manage the learning environment?

What rules and strategies do you implement that are effective or ineffective?

When there is not a set behavior management plan, chaos occurs. Identifying successful classroom management techniques and managing complex behaviors is a tug of war; it will drain the energy from you, but the payoff is invaluable. Pinpoint the hidden agenda of problematic students; get to the meat, or deep-rooted causes of defiant behaviors the student displays, and in return, this can lead to developing specific management strategies that target the child's needs. Identifying the root cause(s) may or may not be beyond your control. Try to speak with the student one on one, outside of class hours. Some students may open up to what the problem is. If they don't open up, don't ignore it. Check personal records to see if there is a consistency of behavior issues. Has the child bounced around from school to school/home to home and doesn't feel safe and secure and is acting out? Are there problems in the home that interfere with the learning environment? Is the student's academic ability on grade level? Or is the child frustrated because the work is too hard or bored because the work is too easy? Speak with school administration and/or counselors; they may be aware of any issues not privy to you.

Managing your class takes strategizing which methods to use. Ironically, all students cannot be treated equally. Knowing your students through building relationships as discussed previously can help you determine how far you can go with students. I knew the students I could chastise and there would be a change in their behavior. I also knew the students I needed to keep my composure, for my sake! It is imperative that you know your students. I once gently chastised a student and ironically, he flipped the script on me! He began yelling, cursing, and he walked out the classroom banging on lockers with his fists and feet; it caused a huge scene and all hell broke loose. I was in total shock and, at first, wanted to retaliate to defend my actions. I had not said or done anything out the ordinary that I hadn't done with any other student. It took several administrators, the principal, the school's resource officer, and the counselor to calm him down. From that day on, I learned the importance of looking into necessary personal records files prior to students arriving and also requesting any Individual Educational Plans (IEP), or Early Intervention Plans (EIP)—the federal special education laws for children with disabilities—or 504 plans, which is the federal civil rights law to stop discrimination against people with disabilities, or any other pertinent information that may help me understand how to deal with a child. Ironically, the student had an intensive record which I was not aware of. He had been identified with Oppositional Defiant Disorder (ODD), an ongoing pattern of uncooperative, defiant, and hostile behavior toward authority figures that seriously interferes with day to day functioning. That day taught me to know my students. I began looking into student records to compile any necessary information that would be helpful for me knowing pertinent information about student backgrounds. In a situation like this, always remain calm. Your first job is to protect yourself and students from potential harm. Don't take outbursts personally. There can be deeper issues that are out of your control, so never take it personally! Let it go and move on. During my observations, I can't tell you how many teachers I've witnessed not even speak to students as they entered their class. A simple greeting can go a long way; it really is common courtesy. Greet students as they enter your classroom. Create a way to address students, whether it is a verbal greeting or a handshake with a simple smile. Whether it was in the morning or during the last period, as students entered, I would always speak to them, calling students by name, even the ones I dreaded coming my way. Yes, I had to force myself many times to put on a fake smile and speak when I didn't want to, but your negative energy won't produce positivity.

Consequences may include	Incentives may include:
• Warning • Detention • Silent lunch • Isolation (in class, time-out chair) • Isolation (sent to another room) • Parent/Guardian contact • Office referral • Revoke privileges (computer time, recess, classroom jobs) • Removal from field trip/event participation • Conference with athletic coach (athletic eligibility may be jeopardized) • Reflective written essay • Teacher-student conference • Behavioral contract	• Verbal praise (private or public, ex: school announcements) • Reward coupon • Student of the Week/Month • Parent contact • Privileges (computer time, music) • Sit where you want for the day, including teacher's desk, bean bag • Edible treats • Line leader • Treasure Chest (choose from a chest of non-edible goodies, ex: school supplies, Dollar Store goodies) • Eat lunch with the teacher • Raffle tickets for end of week class raffle • Coupon (ex: No homework pass) • Class manager • Written positive note to student • Perform a talent for the class • Extra gym/recess time

Figure 6

Establish and reinforce your rules, consequences, and incentives (Figure 6). Reviewing these the first week, as stated previously is necessary, but to be effective, you have to review and update them throughout the school year. New issues may arise as the year progresses, while other rules may not be a priority any longer. Modify them as you see fit. Many times, I have had to instantaneously start off a class period by reviewing my rules, consequences, and incentives. I've even stopped in the middle of class to give an impromptu refresher of classroom expectations when I noticed disruptions that needed immediate attention. It is good practice to schedule time to teach the expectations. Remember, only posting your rules is ineffective.

Minimize your list of rules to no more than five, and switch it from a negative approach into a more positive approach. For example, I can recall my freshman year in high school. My English teacher, who already seemed to hate freshmen, passed out her course syllabus and confirmed my theory. She hated us. It was evident after viewing the page full of rules that began with the words Do Not. It was intimidating. There was honestly an entire page of what we were not to do. It felt so negative and made the class environment uninviting. She had set her tone and maintained it for the entire semester. State your Do Not's in a positive way. "Do not get up without permission" can be changed to a more positive tone. "Raise your hand before getting up." Model your rules. Review them, and practice them with students. Show students the rules don't just tell. I can have a rule that says, Be Respectful, but what it looks like to you may look differently for another student. This is similar to a situation I had; a student whose family used profanity in their daily language. It was used in normal, everyday conversations. But being respectful, for me, meant not blatantly using profanity, especially in front of an adult. So when the student used profanity out loud in conversation, it was normal for her, but I viewed it as disrespectful behavior. I reviewed the expectations of what "respectful" looked and did not look like by setting the norms and creating a behavior matrix (Figure 7). This can be adjusted to fit any grade level. Students got a chance to interact with the rules and provide examples of what each rule should look like. These were teachable moments as we role played and had engaging, deep conversations. Students were excited to share their own experiences. Students could better understand my rules and expectations. Researchers have revealed that the more transparent and clear teachers are about their behavioral expectations, the more successful students are in meeting those expectations (Evertson, Emmer, & Worsham, 2006; Zirpoli, 2008). Remember, more rules does not equate to good behavior.

	LOCATION		
Behavior	Classroom	Hallway/Transitions	Cafeteria
Be Respectful	• Speak when addressed • Honor personal space • Ask before touching • Arrive to class on time	• Wash your hands • Honor everyone's private moments • Walk on the correct side of the hallway • Keep traffic flowing without stopping in the middle	• Say please and thank you • Use your inside voice • Throw away your trash
Be Prepared	• Have learning tools such as writing utensils, notebooks, and paper	• Use lockers at the designated time • Get all needed class materials	• Have monies and lunch money ready before getting to the register
Follow Directions	• Use assigned websites • Respond to directions the first time	• Adhere to any adult's directives	• Enter the lunch line on the correct side • Adhere to all lunch monitors' directives

Figure 7

Create a Comfortable Class

First and foremost, make your classroom feel inviting. I've visited classes and have felt uncomfortable. Some have felt like prison walls; the class was bare with hardly anything on the walls. It wasn't warm nor inviting. Then I've been to some classes which have felt like a hoarder's sanctuary. Less can be more, but not enough feels empty. Vincent (1999) states, "Effective teachers focus on organizing furnishings and materials in order to facilitate instruction in several general ways: (1) student seating should be easy to monitor by the teacher and not distracting to the students; (2) well-used areas of the room should be easily accessible; and (3) materials and equipment should be quite accessible by students and the teacher." Creating a warm environment can create a sense of safety for students. Create ambience. Incorporate lamps, decorative lights, and light-scented plug-ins, if allowed, to add personality. Be mindful of students' sensitivity to florescent and bright lighting. When decorating, be diverse in choosing pictures and wall decorations. Include all cultures and all types of people, including those in wheelchairs, obese, thin, wearing glasses, or tall or short stature. Create your classroom atmosphere, clutter-free.

Be strategic how you set up your student desks and know your school's expectations. One of my principals required cooperative groups of four to five, so my class was set up accordingly. I thought one seating arrangement would work and often realized it didn't; it became a trial and error. Sometimes changing seating with particular students is necessary. If it is your discretion, keep in mind the different personalities you may have during one class period and whether they should be in groups, pairs, or independent. Creating a classroom seating arrangement with a variety of seating options (pairs, individual/rows, and groups) within one setting is ideal; the physical arrangement influences the efficacy of instruction. Your content needs to also be taken under consideration. A science class—since there are labs to conduct—may be structured differently than a history class, which may include more cooperative groups for discussions. Additionally, students' learning preferences and needs should be accommodated. One student may need to be allowed freedom of movement while another student may like a quiet, calm work space. Keep your class flexible. It may change per curriculum and activity to accommodate teaching and learning. Take into consideration that you should be able to circulate freely throughout the room.

Take gender into consideration as well. When I taught single-gender classes, my male students were very active; although my classes were smaller, I had to make it spacious enough for them to move freely during learning activities. My female students appreciated cooperative groups; they engaged in more discussions with each other, so closeness wasn't a major problem. However, don't limit your setting; remember, the key is to be flexible. Routine is necessary, however; for older students, changing seating arrangements ever so often is good. Students are allowed to work with different students and are not stuck in the same seat all semester. Be considerate to students' seating requests. Some performed better independently and would state that as I made seating arrangements. Take all types of learners into consideration.

Develop a Simple Behavior Management Plan

Teachers can eradicate many behavior problems by establishing an effective behavior plan. Solicit the assistance of colleagues to develop and reinforce a plan. Having a management plan for your class is good, but there is power in a unified effort with colleagues; it becomes more effective when everyone "looks the same." Create a plan by teams, grade level, or school-wide. Usually, schools have school-wide reform, where a one-size-fits-all discipline plan is in place; however, if there is not one, tackle the discipline issues by creating your own. Even if you don't have all team members on board, you are the captain of your ship. Close your door and make your plan work for you. It is always good practice to speak with school leaders or your evaluator about your discipline plan implementation. They are more likely to be back you if your decisions are ever challenged by other school personnel or a parent. We, teachers, seem to focus on the negative and overlook all the positivity that occurs right in front of us. After creating your behavior matrix, establish procedures, consequences, and rewards. These are only as effective as you make them. The results of a meta-analysis of research on classroom management practices indicate that when teachers use effective behavior management techniques, students exhibit less disruptive, inappropriate, and aggressive behavior than do students whose teachers do not use such techniques. (Oliver, Wehby & Reschley, 2011)

What is your procedure for student use of electronic devices such as a cellphone during class? If students don't follow the procedures, what is the consequence? How is the consequence enforced? Remember, your rules will only be as effective as you make them. You give some an inch, they'll take a mile. If you set your tone from the beginning, the problems will be minimal. This reverts back to building a strong relationship with students. Review for procedures for classroom arrival and dismissal, submitting work, locker uses, and restroom breaks, just to name a few. Apply your consequences meaningfully in order for them to curtail a repeat. Consequences should range in intensity. A first offender, who didn't bring supplies, should not receive an office referral for administrative disciplinary action. However, a physical altercation between students may be an instant office referral. Develop your class plan by hierarchy. The offense numbers may vary. For example (Figure 8):

5 Step Discipline Plan	
1st Offense	Warning
2nd Offense	Teacher-Student Conference
3rd Offense	Parent Contact
4th Offense	Silent Lunch/Detention
5th Offense	Office referral

Figure 8

Please note that it is common for students to be upset when issued a consequence. When issuing out offense levels, be firm, give eye contact, remain gentle and calm, and most importantly, watch your tone. You may have to ignore a student who is retaliating in order to not disrupt the class flow. Refrain from embarrassing students and calling them out in front of their peers by openly stating their consequence. This could open Pandora's Box. If you have an inclination to how the student may respond, wait until after class to address the student and issue their consequence away from the masses. This is why knowing your students really comes into play.

Next, what is your system for recognizing students? Instead of entering the classroom and recognizing negative behavior by identifying what students are doing wrong, reward the positive. After I would stand at my door and greet students during transition, I would give out raffle-like tickets to students who were on task. I didn't have to say a word; I was seen and not heard. It's amazing at how the positive will overshadow the negative. Use reinforcements such as an extrinsic reward or praise. This encourages positive behavior in hopes that students will be self-motivated to do the right thing because it's simply the right thing to do. Don't go broke spending money on trinkets. Rewarding students does not equate to buying them things. Verbal recognition such as "good job" or "right on" goes a long way. Contact parents, send postcards and notes home, allow extra computer time, or give more privileges. Students will appreciate this more than ever. You can even allow your students the option of choosing their reward! The older students are, the more teachers shy away from these things. Just as we like to be recognized as Teacher of the Month, Teacher of the Year, and other recognitions, students need this as well.

Students should be taught and reminded of the plan they are expected to follow. The consequences and incentives should be visibly posted for students at all times. At various intervals throughout the school year, revisit them with students so they are always reminded of your expectations, and remember, your plan is only as effective as you make it.

A Student Can Spoil the Entire Class Environment. What to Do?

I will admit, I took great pleasure when misbehaved students were absent. I just needed a day off from them, but my most challenging students seemed to be at school every day! Problem students don't care about their own learning or the learning of others. Although you can't control their behavior, control your class. Asking the student to move to another seat or get quiet may not go in your favor. If they are disruptive, they are more than likely to be defiant to any of your requests. However, once you get the students started on their assignment, quietly ask the child if you can speak to him or her in the hallway. Whether the child moves or not, don't disrupt the entire class period for one; you may have to bite the bullet and leave it alone at that moment. However, make contact with a parent immediately whether it makes a difference or not, and, in extreme cases, request for administration if the negative behavior persists.

We don't want to give students the choice to opt out of their learning. However, you may experience excessive disruptive students who couldn't give two cents if you started teaching today, tomorrow, next month, or next year. After you've done all you can, teach to students who want to learn, but never change your expectation. I've had to do it. I stated to the class, "those who want to learn, gather in a designated spot" and I kept the show moving. I allowed students to be the captain of their own ship; their decision to make. The students who were disruptive became defensive when I continued to teach over them. A few even walked out, only to return later after I informed the office of their disappearing act. Fortunately, the problem students were known by administration, so their behavior was no surprise. However, looking back, there was a behavior plan in place, but it was inconsistently used so its effectiveness was weak. I'm positive if it was used consistently, my outcome would have been better. Did that change the behavior of students from that point on? Of course not; however my ultimate concern was to do what I was charged to do—teach. Things did progress along the way, and at the end one student was removed for possession of opioids, and afterwards the class dynamic drastically improved.

However, before it gets extreme, try these methods:

- Assign students leadership roles: Transition their negative energy into a positive role.
- Be fair: If students feel they are treated unjustly, they are more likely to retaliate. Make sure to not show favoritism.
- Be prepared: Have "just in case" strategies on hand for volatile situations. (ie., have a designated teacher's class where you can send the students for a cool-off period)
- Stay private: Calling kids out will only backfire. Embarrassing students only strokes your ego and will not change the situation. Don't threaten them with what

you plan on doing. Threatening students by saying such things like, "I'm going to write you up!" holds no water with an already disgruntled student. In fact, it will trigger the anger.
- Empathize with students: Figure out what is going on outside of class. There has to be a deeper issue. Request the student to stay after class to talk, or refer the student to the school's counselor.
- Know when to walk away: I've had to pretend as if students were extinct. I could hear him or her talk in retaliation of me, but I refused to engage. If the student senses that weakness, they will ignite the fire. Don't stop the whole class for a few knuckleheads. Continue on teaching to the students who are attentive.
- Change class periods: Seek administration's assistance to break up cliques of problematic students who are in the same class together. Some students fit well into the phrase, "monkey see, monkey do." They are disruptive because they want to show out in front of their friends. Splitting them up may be the difference.
- Incorporate your incentive program: This is only effective if the incentives are what students want. No matter what the grade level, it works every time. Recognize small achievements.
- Give chances: Always expect good behavior. I have been guilty of making a student stay outside in the hallway and refused entrance because I just knew they would be disruptive that day. They didn't do anything, but I called myself being proactive to make my day better. I labeled them as "the bad student" and that is exactly what I got. Just as we need more chances to improve, allow students the same privilege.

- Don't give up…yet: Exhaust all possible avenues for your student; unfortunately, everyone can't be helped. It may be simply out of your control. Get administration, parents, and counselors involved. Additionally, keep well-documented anecdotal records; you never know when they will come in handy.
- Self-reflect: Ask yourself, Have I been fair? Could I have done or said anything to rub the student the wrong way? Have I tried to connect with the student? Could I do anything more to change the relationship?

Teaching in the 21st Century

Twenty-first-century teaching is a phenomenon! There is a radical difference in how kids want and need to learn today than in yesterday's traditional classes. Even my teaching practices a decade ago are so much different than now. Teaching the basics are no longer enough to reach today's children. There is no one-size-fits-all instruction. I once had a social studies teacher in middle school that all the students were terrified of. Looking back, she had us in check! We never spoke out and were too afraid to raise our hand, let alone get out of our seats. That's how she wanted it, and that's how it was. There was no student interactions, engaging lessons, cooperative groups, or partners. We sat independently with our desks in rows every single day. There was only one way to sit, and that was forward. We dreaded being called upon to answer a question, fearing we may not know the answer, which would result in being scolded and embarrassed. I remember that class like yesterday. Every day, students sat and listened, lecture style. It was teacher-focused, not student-focused. We all hated her and her class! This class setting may seem ideal, and every once in a while I reminisce and wish my class mimicked hers, but when I come back to reality, to be impactful, this type of teacher in the inner city can't exist anymore because it simply doesn't work. Try that method if you want (or can), and I can guarantee the results will not be your intended outcome. There is a difference between being firm and unreasonably strict.

The goal of having effective classroom management strategies is to eliminate distractions that threaten the flow of instruction. The fact of the matter is, in a class where disruptions occur frequently, the learning environment is threatened. Disruptive behavior in any classroom impedes learning, and the time spent in redirecting students back takes valuable instruction time, which in turn affects student academic performance. (Musti-Rao & Haydon, 2011, pp.91-92). We want students to be self-motivated to learn, therefore, having a solid plan in place takes strategic planning and is necessary. One of the strongest weapons against classroom management is engagement. Make classroom management a solid, consistent effort and plan engaging lessons from bell to bell that allows no leeway for disruptions. Managing a class of adolescents and teens has its challenges. Everyone has bad days, including students and educators, but having subpar classroom management is non-negotiable for the success of your class. We've all been irritated and have maybe had a pinch of thought of walking away from it all. Just know why you're in it and who needs you most. Revisit your philosophy of education; that is your reason. You can go home to your cozy home, but it is a possibility that some of your students may not be getting a hot meal or going to a warm home. Don't focus on the negative, but instead highlight the positives and let that be your motivation.

Methods that Work

It is true that discipline is a critical factor affecting the inner city. Despite this fact, schools are cutting back on assigning in-school and out-of-school suspensions in hopes of finding alternatives to students missing valuable instructional time and preventing reoccurrences. Unfortunately, although students are suspended, research does not support its effectiveness; usually, there are repeat offenders, and they return to the class displaying identical behaviors and falling behind academically. Students who are occupied in instruction are less likely to have behavior problems (Greenwood, Horton, & Utley, 2002; Sutherland & Oswald, 2005; Sutherland & Wehby, 2001). Too many discipline referrals is a red flag to school administrators to your classroom management practices and class environment; it negatively impacts you. So how can we help remedy this? Create optimal learning opportunities that eliminates negative behaviors and magnifies student learning opportunities by adopting and adapting the following ten classroom techniques and approaches for any grade level and content area:

1. **You've Got Mail.** Be open to student concerns by incorporating a mailbox where students can discreetly tell you of any issues arising. Students can be scared or ashamed to verbally tell you of any issues, such as bullying. They don't want to be known as a snitch. A mailbox allows students to open up to you and make you aware of the happenings in your class. Check your mailbox daily and discover issues students may be experiencing. Students may have stated they were the only one working on their group assignment or that they desired a seat change, or you may be alerted to an altercation that may happen in the restroom later on. Make sure to station it where

students aren't able to check it. Students will appreciate this opportunity, and it continues to build trust from you.

2. **Student Leaders.** Bring order to your class by assigning classroom managers, such as a restroom manager, an errand manager, a timer, and a distributer for leadership opportunities. It works on all grade levels and content areas. Managers should change weekly to allow everyone to have a chance. Students like to be the boss. They take ownership, and by doing a good job, students get a chance to earn incentives such as sit in the teacher's desk, preferential seating, no-homework passes, tangible items, listen to music while working, computer time, etc. Students would really take control of their jobs; even when I forgot to do something, my managers would always remember. For elementary, you may assign roles daily or every other day. Ironically, high school students will be more prone to take part in the roles as well.

3. **Teamwork Makes the Dream Work.** I've shied away from grouping students during work time because the work wasn't distributed evenly. Certain students would carry the load while others did little to nothing even though they were receiving same grade. This can be solved by using Cooperative Group Role Cards (Figure 12). Teams work better when there are defined responsibilities to each designated role. For teams of three to five, assign roles such as a leader, presenter, time manager, scriber etc. This will allow all students to contribute to the group. Everyone will be responsible for bringing "something to the table." Change up student roles often; it'll give all group members an opportunity to experience each role. Make the role's characteristics clear so that every student understands the expectation. Their roles are only as powerful as you make them. They will interactively

learn, and learn from each other. Place the role cards on the desk, or keep a supply basket where students can retrieve materials. Your roles should be dependent on the assignment's objective.

4. **Give Power.** Empower students who pose a threat to the learning environment to your advantage. They are going to use that energy anyway, so why not put it to use—for you! Reverse negative behavior by relinquishing your authority to them. They can become the help you need. Reposition them at your desk to work technology such as controlling the Smart board or going to the next slide on a Prezi presentation. Allow them to be the group leader. Let them assist you with straightening up your shelf or overseeing that students clean up their area before transitioning, or allow them to distribute and collect papers. The goal is to make them feel important; show them their help is needed and wanted. If trusted, allow them to run an errand every once in a while; this will show them that you trust them. It will be easier to discipline them if needed. Sporadically provide small incentives to show your appreciation.

5. **Redirecting Made Easy.** Create a whole class redirecting strategy that is more effective than yelling over them to be quiet and attentive. When I was a student in school, I can recall my teachers slamming the door to demand our attention; eventually the glass on the door cracked. As an adult with my own class, that method never appealed to me and brings more distraction to other classes. Clapping or chants are simple, but powerful. For example, if students could hear my voice, I would tell them to clap a number of times, or they would repeat after me orally. For example, " If you can hear my voice, clap once. If you can hear my voice, clap twice. If you can hear my voice, clap

three times," Speak in a regular tone; the goal is not to have to raise your voice. Even if a few students responded at one, by the third time, I always had the entire class's attention. Make this into a routine, so no matter if you are in or outside the classroom, students are familiar with your expectation. Create your own redirection call—that may be more familiar to students—that you have taken from a popular song, or Teacher states while raising his/her hand, "When my hand is up," Students respond, "My mouth is closed." Repeat as necessary. But remember, the goal is to eliminate yelling.

6. **Pair, Then Share.** Have you ever been in a meeting or workshop and the facilitator randomly called on people for answers or feedback? It's the worst feeling ever. You want to hide or excuse yourself to the nearest restroom to avoid it. You can be caught off guard. You may not have enough time to process your thoughts, and you want to make sure you answer the question accurately to avoid embarrassment. I was one for calling on students, especially the ones who weren't paying attention, and the tables were turned when it happened to me. Allowing students to share their answers and ideas with a partner prior to calling on them builds confidence or self-esteem. They will also put more effort into their activities, stay on task, and build an understanding of the material. Allow students the opportunity to collaborate with a partner, a neighbor, or group. Then, call on a student and their confidence and conceptual understanding of the topic will be enhanced. Make sure they start off by stating, "My partner/group discussed…"

7. **Exit 1, 2, 3, 4.** "The bell does not dismiss you, I dismiss you!" This is how it should go, but right after a bell sounds, how do your students assemble out the door? In my

experiences, on more than one occasion, a student was trampled because students tried to rush out the door at one time. It was unnecessary; injuries could have been avoided if a proper procedure was in place. One helpful strategy is when I say, "One!" all students gather their belongings, but not get out of their seat. When I say "Two!" all students should stand at their desk. When "Three" is said, predetermine which half of the class will leave first and allow them to exit, and at "Four," all students should be exiting the door. This will make exiting orderly. Note: To make dismissal more exciting for smaller children, call students to leave more creatively, such as, say, "If you have on red shoes, you are excused. If your last name begins with an S, you are excused. If you were dropped off in a car this morning, you are excused. If you have a sibling that attends this school, you are excused." However, try this with older children; you'd be surprised at their reaction and participation!

8. **Student Lead Lessons/Debates.** Engaging lessons are key components to classroom management. Allowing students to take lead in presenting a lesson holds their interest, and students make a personal investment in their learning. I tried this strategy after collaborating with several colleagues from a national conference I attended; it became part of my yearly instructional plans from then on. The idea sounded good, but I was skeptical that it would work with my dynamic of students. Of course it would work with *their* dynamic of students, they have students totally unlike mine, I thought. I would be doing all the work anyway; however, I was pleasantly surprised. I never thought my students would or could deliver such an assignment. By allowing students the autonomy to deliver the lesson, providing optional resources to use,

and allowing in-class time to collaborate with their partners, students delivered the assignment better than I expected. This method is an effective way for students to demonstrate their mastery level; it promotes collaboration with peers, and it develops critical thinking skills.They present information in a way that is new and exciting to their peers.

a. **Assign students a specific topic from your content:** Material can be a new skill/topic or a review.

b. **Provide the guidelines:** Include a brief lesson plan template (Figure 9). Usually two to three days are provided, but it may depend on the assignment's complexity. Review the rubric.

c. **Determine progress:** Check for understanding as students work. Review and collect material that may need copying as their handout. Review their presentation and aid when needed.

d. **Student Lead Lesson:** Aid with the flow of their lesson (Figure 9). If you need to chime in, do so to reiterate or clarify a point or to ask more in-depth questions for the class.

Student nervousness will improve with time. Continuing to provide leadership opportunities will build their confidence. After the lesson, students should reflect on their performance to self-assess so they can improve (see Figure 10).

Note: As this becomes regular practice, for humor, and for students to get a feel of "teacher blues," I would often emulate student behaviors such as blurting out and talking to others while the teacher talked. Students got a kick out of it and really see teaching from our perspective.

ACHIEVING SUCCESS IN INNER CITY SCHOOLS

Student-Teacher Lesson Plan

Lesson

Date to teach:

Name(s)

What will you be teaching:

Materials Needed:

How will you begin the lesson?

What fun activity will you do? Quizziz, Kahoot, Game, Online Game Other:

Web Links?

What type of presentation are you doing? Prezi, PowerPoint, Animoto, Other:

What questions will you ask students before, during, and after the lesson? (Do not use begin sentences with "What")

Question 1:

Question 2:

Question 3:

Question 4:

Teacher Approval:

Figure 9

Student nervousness will improve with time. Continuing to provide leadership opportunities will build their confidence. After the lesson, students should reflect on their performance for a self-assessment so they can improve (see Figure 10).

Note: As this becomes regular practice, for humor, and for students to get a feel of "teacher blues," I would often emulate student behaviors such as blurting out and talking to others while the teacher talked. Students got a kick out of it and really see teaching from our perspective.

9. **No Pencil, No Paper, No Technology Day.** Twenty-first-century teaching is not the standard teaching that took place a decade ago. Boost student engagement by incorporating "No Pencil, No Paper" day; it takes planning and creativity, but the results are awesome. Students will not recognize learning is taking place. The only rule is just as it says; students need to bring nothing but themselves to class that day. How can you plan a lesson in a fun way that will capture and hold all students' attention? What games, besides interactive computer games, can you create where there is more teacher-student interaction versus student-computer interaction? This is different than a technology day where students are on the computer. Try some suggested activities that can be adjusted to fit any grade level or content area. The learning outcome should drive the activities.

- **Academic Tic Tac Toe:** Played like the original game. Create a tic-tac-toe poster board or use floor tape to create a board. Use index cards to write down the review questions, or use prewritten resources for this activity. Divide students into small groups to play, or play as a class; one side are X's, the others are O's. If the student on the X team answers correctly, place an X on the board. If not, the O team must answer correctly to steal the square. If they get it right, place the O anywhere, if not, use this as a teaching

Student Teacher Reflection Sheet

How would you rate your lesson?

      1   2   3   4   5

What do you believe went well?

How could you have improved?

Would you want to teach the class again? Why or why not?

Figure 10

moment to clear up misconceptions. It will still be the O team's move. (They took the other team's question, so it's now their turn). Repeat until three X's and three O's have been made horizontally or vertically. Note: Adapt as needed, or create your own rules. Use as a reinforcement to a recently learned skill or as review before a test. The only goal is to make learning fun! You'll be surprised at how all students participate, even the ones who you didn't think would.

- **Musical Chairs with a Twist:** This fun and exciting interactive activity will motivate all learners and eliminate off-task behavior. This activity is similar to musical chairs, a game in which students move around a group of chairs as music is being played; when the music stops, each student sits in a chair. Students will rotate around chairs in a single file line as the music plays. (Every other desk/chair should be turned the opposite direction.) 1. Have one less chair than there are students. 2. Play the music (no more than 20 seconds), then stop it randomly. 3. As the music stops, students will scurry to find an empty chair; the one who is still standing must answer the review question. 4. Remove one chair after each round, and the game is repeated until there is a winner. If a student gets it right, allow them to explain further. If a student gets the answer incorrect, use it as a teachable moment. Play this game as a review, with text dependent questions, to memorize state capitals, to identify scientific terms, or to solve math problems. Be sure you make all rules clear and monitor closely.
- **Charades:** This interactive activity is played similar to the original game. This activity gives students an alternative way to act out different characters from a book you're reading, key events from history, or important

body functions. This is a good way to introduce a topic or a unit review. 1. Gather a list of terms that will be used and write them on index cards. 2. Split students into two teams. 3. Students from each team will randomly take turns to "perform" while their other team members must state what they are acting out. Allow each "performer" to randomly select an index card. No other person is allowed to see it. They cannot speak or write the word or definition, and allow each a moment to plan how he or she will act it out. The first group to guess the correct word wins a point. To help keep the groups from shouting out random words, you can deduct a point for each incorrect guess. The goal is to make sure they understand the material you taught.

- **Say, Word?:** Enjoy this highly interactive activity played similarly to the popular game Taboo. Even your more reserved students are sure to get involved. This activity assesses student knowledge, builds vocabulary, and uses listening, speaking, and collaboration skills. Create index cards to cover the topic. Write the main word at the top, and underneath, write at least four related words. (Figure 11). The goal of the game is for the speaker to get the teammates to guess the main word. Allow one minute for each team. Procedures:

   a. Split the class into teams. It is preferable to have two to four teams of no more than eight.
   b. Teams will rotate speakers from their team and an overseer from the opposite team. The overseer will sit next to the speaker of the opposing team to make sure none of the related words are mentioned. If the related word is mentioned, no point can be earned.

c. Position the speaker so that the team members cannot see the words on the Taboo cards.
d. A team gets a point for every card that they guess correctly.

Note: No gestures, no sounds, and using any part of the main or related words are prohibited. Ex: if the word is horseman, the speaker cannot use "man" to give clues, no sounds like, rhyming with words.

* cut each card to form a stack *

CARD 1 Precipitation	CARD 2 Theme	CARD 3 Adolf Hitler	CARD 4 Square
Rain	Big Idea	Germany	Four
Weather	thoughts	Jew	Parallel
Sleet	lesson	Concentration Camp	Equal
Evaporation	literature	Anne Frank	Quadrilateral
Wet	moral	Nazi	Same

Figure 11

For Card 1, the presenter can't mention any of the related words; however he or she can help his or her team guess the correct word by saying:

1. It's part of the water cycle.
5. It falls to the ground.
6. It includes drizzle or hail.

5. Competitions: Healthy competition and participation pushes participants to excel! Don't shy away from incorporating it. Keep the competition fair with students of similar abilities. Include team captains (they were always used to help keep the group on task). Remember, as you create healthy, engaging competitions, the ultimate goal is that students are eager to learn. It will definitely boost student engagement and motivation.

No matter which strategies are employed, teachers play a massive role in their effectiveness. The aforementioned techniques foster an engaging, safe learning environment and reinforce positive behavior. Implement those that work for your population of students.

Supporting a Positive, Social Learning Environment

Students need positive expectations from teachers in order to be motivated. It is a true misconception that a quiet classroom equates to good classroom management. The best types of learning occurs when there is student-to-student interaction and student-to-teacher interaction. Should learning be active or passive? Active! Social interaction includes deep conversations during lessons where students are questioning, experimenting, and collaborating with each other; this results in a positive learning environment. Classrooms with a positive social environment tend to foster students' sense of belongingness, enjoyment, enthusiasm, and respect towards others (Wentzel et al., 2010). This is when productivity takes place; a manageable and orderly environment is evident when this occurs. Not only are students engaged in learning, but also their social needs are being met. How teachers provide support to students and facilitate peer relations in the

COOPERATIVE GROUP ROLE CARDS	
TEAM LEADER • You are responsible for making sure everyone does his/her part. • Ask if everyone understands the task. • Notify the teacher if there are any questions or concerns. • You are to work collaboratively with your group.	**TIME MANAGER** • You are responsible for keeping all time constraints. • Keep your team on pace to make sure the assignment is completed before time is called. • You are to work collaboratively with your group.
PRESENTER • You will present the group's work when called. • You must stand and speak clearly and confidently. • You are to work collaboratively with your group.	**SCRIBER** • You are responsible for writing down or typing the assignment. • Make sure to get everyone's input. • You are to work collaboratively with your group.
EDITOR • You are responsible for editing all work before submitting. • Make sure the work is legible after viewing it from the scriber. • Be sure everyone's name is visible on the work, and it is written in correct format. (MLA, APA) • You are to work collaboratively with your group.	**ILLUSTRATOR** • You are responsible for the illustrations of this task. Make sure to follow the directions of the assignment. • Make it colorful, if required. • You are to work collaboratively with your group.
NOISE CONTROLLER • You are responsible for controlling the noise level in your group. • Make sure one person speaks at a time as you share ideas. • You are to work collaboratively with your group.	**ASSEMBLER** • You are the only one allowed to get out of your seat (sharpen a pencil, retrieve material and return material). • Make sure you know all the material the group will need. • You are to work collaboratively with your group.

Figure 12

classroom has effects on students' academic and social outcomes (Merrit et al., 2012; Patrick; Sakiz, Pape, & Woolfolk Hoy, 2012). Provide a range of opportunities for social interaction during learning to promote autonomy while sharing meaningful ideas. Students enjoy socializing, so why not incorporate it into everyday instruction. The truth is, they are going to talk despite it being class time or not, but have the power to control what they are discussing and how their conversations develop.

Feelings, the physical and mental response to emotion, are what can hamper or promote attention. And attention—or the ability to avoid distraction—is necessary for learning (Weiss, 2000). Social issues such as those on social media, students' personal relationships, and happenings within or outside of the community will definitely spill over into the classroom. How will you handle this to keep the learning environment positive? You must address this or even incorporate it into your lessons. As students continue to trust the learning environment, they will feel more comfortable speaking openly about issues that are near and dear to them. For example, the social media frenzy is here to stay. When students bring conflicts from online into the classroom, use it as a teachable moment that fits your grade level. Ask students what is the less problematic way to solve the problem and discuss it. Create a scenario and have them act it out. Or, make it into a debate that fits your subject. For math, make sure students focus of the facts involving numbers/statistics, or for history, make sure they conduct research on the topic and present their findings.

Websites such as Kidblog provide a safe way for students to publish their writing while teachers can monitor the activity and approve or disapprove of postings. Teach students how to disagree respectfully while being appropriate and thoughtful of feelings because some will only mimic the negativity they witness online such as profanity-laced comments and attacks when there is a disagreement. Teacher-monitored blogging will allow students to express themselves in a safe way. The truth is that when a person's mind is occupied on outside factors, it blocks their learning ability. "Emotion drives attention, which drives learning" (Sylwester, 2000). How you feel determines how well you learn. Therefore, create a safe haven to address issues; students will appreciate you for it.

No Supplies, No Problem

Students may come to your class without supplies, and some may not even care if they have them or not. I was always flabbergasted by students, especially car riders, who were dropped off by parents or guardians in the morning and got out of the car without anything in hand. Didn't students and parents know the child was headed to school? A place where pens, pencils, and notebook paper were necessities to be successful? In some cases, it wasn't that students didn't have supplies at home or in their lockers, but there were just some who would choose the days they would bring them. I had to choose my battles very quickly. For years, I would refuse to hand out any materials to students. My job was to teach them, so the least students could do was bring supplies, right? The negative in this is that students become troublemakers when they aren't doing anything. However, when students have an opportunity to get writing tools, most will. If some students can get away with not doing anything, and unfortunately, some will try it without hesitation, reiterate your rules and expectations, and don't allow students to opt out of learning.

As teachers, we spend countless amounts of dollars purchasing materials for our classes, from tape dispensers to copy paper and even clocks to place on the wall. Save your money on notebook paper and writing utensils because supplies are right there in your class, in the hallways, and all around the building. Implement a "Lost Pencil Cup." Daily, collectively, students left pencils, pens, and highlighters on the floor. I could walk down the hallway and see a pencil, and it would be now the property of my class. They would be added to my "Lost Pencil Cup," a metal mesh cup I bought from the Dollar store and now labeled as such. Students would then be allowed to get a pencil as needed. To maintain your supply, use a collateral rule. This will guarantee that there is a writing utensil available for every class each day. Students would exchange a shoe, a notebook, their jacket, or something of value in exchange for a writing utensil from the cup. In the same way, create a "Lost Paper Folder" where students are able to retrieve paper when needed. Students leave unclaimed notebooks and notebook paper around. Place a folder on the wall or in a designated area. Set your limit to how many sheets a students can take. To make this more manageable, assign a manager for each. Also, advocate for your classroom and solicit aid from neighboring companies and communities who may donate boxes of class materials for students. However, keep enforcing your rules to ensure students come prepared, but don't let that interfere with the learning environment. One of my favorite poems by Joshua T. Dickerson says it best:

> I woke myself up
> Because we ain't got an alarm clock
> Dug in the dirty clothes basket,
> Cause ain't nobody washed my uniform
> Brushed my hair and teeth in the dark,
> Cause the lights ain't on
> Even got my baby sister ready,
> Cause my mama ain't home.
> Got both of us to school on time,
> To get us a good breakfast.

Then when I got to class the teacher fussed
Cause I ain't got no pencil.

Rewards, Not Bribes

Of course we want students to be intrinsically motivated; however, there is nothing wrong with tangible rewards such as snacks, no-homework coupons, computer time, preferential seating, etc., as long as it is not bribing. It is bribing if a teacher states, "If you stay quiet/do your work, I will give you this reward." This reward is a quick fix and takes away from students' intrinsic motivation. The student, in this situation, holds the power. The student may now only perform if there is "pay" that comes along with it. It will become an ongoing pattern and difficult to break. A reward, on the other hand, is when students earn the incentive by already doing the right thing; it reinforces appropriate behavior and promotes personal motivation. A teacher giving an award may state, "Good job! You met your reading goal this week." One former colleague spent countless amounts of money bribing students to behave. It was an everyday thing, no joke. Every day, students would leave with pickles, chips, candy, etc. Students even came out the class with peanut butter and jelly sandwiches! It was a temporary fix and students started to only behave positively when they knew they were getting something in return. This is not the right message to send to your students. Reward, but don't bribe.

Have rewards that students want. Treasure chests are effective for all grade levels. For more health conscious treats, introduce more nutritious snacks. I never realized how much students would be interested in celery and blue cheese or granola bars as rewards until I witnessed it firsthand. It, ironically, worked for a science teacher who decided that adding more sugar and junk to kids' diets wasn't her thing. Honestly, I was convinced that students would not want her healthy snack. I just knew students would definitely not buy into it, but they did, time and time again. Recognize positive behavior regularly. Some students need immediate recognition. Long-term incentives for them are too long, and students lose interest of the goals when they can't see the end in mind. Try weekly or bi-weekly recognitions. Don't always reward the same students. Stretch the qualifications to fit those who may not be the usual honorees, it may pull others in. Keep in mind that rewards don't have to be tangible. For the student who met their reading goal, allow them to choose their next book. A student who has achieved a higher score on an assignment can become a peer helper/mentor or teach a mini-lesson.

Teaching Methods and Strategies

Tell me, I forget; teach me, I remember; involve me, and I will learn.

—BENJAMIN FRANKLIN

THERE IS NOTHING more rewarding than monitoring academic growth and actually seeing students progress; on the same note, there is nothing more devastating than pouring your heart out while planning lessons and teaching, only for students to not make any academic progress. When I first started teaching in 2005 my state's standardized test provided three levels of achievement: exceeds, meets, or did not meet. The test, for over a decade, did not genuinely allow teachers to determine their effectiveness over one academic school year, although most assumed it did. Teachers whose students passed were deemed effective, while teachers whose students' scores did not meet the state standards were deemed ineffective. This false sense of achievement, or failure, for teachers, parents, and students provided a minimum-competency level and did not determine how much students grew academically within the full school year. For years, unfortunately, it was the determining factor to students being promoted or retained, and teacher evaluation measurement outcomes depended on it. For years, I contemplated transferring to a school where students were guaranteed to at least pass the state's standardized test. It would make my job much more simple. I wouldn't have to give planning and teaching as much effort as with students who had a greater chance of failing or passing, or so I thought. But what if all teachers thought this way and acted upon their thoughts? Teaching in inner city will make you sharpen your craft. I learned so much about the essence of teaching and learning by reading literature, signing up for workshops, collaborating with colleagues near and far, joining organizations that were specific to my content, and I was committed to doing all I could to help close the achievement gap for the students I directly touched. These were my children and I couldn't give up on them just to make it easier for me. Some districts continue to measure teacher effectiveness by a pass or fail system; however, this does not determine their impact on students; this doesn't tell the full story of how much value was added. Of course, as human beings, we want to always see a passing grade of A's, B's, and C's; however, don't let that be a sole measurement of your impact; focus on the academic growth. Monitoring the growth will most accurately provide a true depiction (reliability) of how much students achieved over time.

Teaching techniques and strategies have a great impact on student learning and achievement. Before effective teaching and learning can occur, however, its prerequisite is having solid classroom management techniques to produce an environment that is conducive to learning. Success and failures can be attributed to what teachers teach and their delivery methods. Students learn best when they are engaged, supported, and feel that lessons are relevant to their lives. When students ask, "Why does this matter?" teachers need to be ready with credible answers that connect the students' interest, goals, and identity (Corso, Bundick, Quaglia, & Haywood, 2013). Students need to understand "why." I used to get offended when students asked why an assignment had to be done, as if they were just being obnoxious when they inquired as to the importance of certain lessons. I realized that students weren't being obnoxious but genuinely wanted to know the relevance of the content to their everyday lives. Students have a great curiosity and need for understanding; therefore, stating beforehand why the content matters will provide insight for them and will alleviate you of the "why does this matter" questions that are sure to come.

Students must be provided with challenging opportunities to explore, create, and participate in in-depth conversations, including debates with their peers to optimize their learning. Modern education, no matter the academic level, should not be structured as a sit-and-get. A singular mode of instruction is ineffective, repetitive, and boring. Student performance increases when there is a span of instructional approaches that support their needs. Engaging instruction that involves all students and supports their individual strengths is important. There are hundreds of instructional strategies that can be used by teachers specific to content, grade level, and ability. However, the strategies discussed in this chapter are researched best strategies and can be implemented by all, no matter the grade level. We must teach through a rigorous and challenging curriculum that is enriched with a variety of tools. They [teachers] must teach on purpose— knowing what to teach, why teach it, how to teach it, and how to assess students' level of understanding. Tailored instruction to meet the needs of all students will enable participation to the fullest extent possible and progress to increasingly higher levels of expertise (Braund & Reiss, 2004). This happens when there is sufficient planning and a variety of resources.

  Practice using an instructional pacing guide per your content to better your structure lessons. An instructional pacing guide can be referred to as a scope and sequence, framework, or curriculum map. Developing units, using essential questions (Wiggens & McTighe, 2005), and inquiry-based learning approaches (Levy,

Thomas, Drago, & Rex, 2013) can help teachers making learning authentic for students. This is critical to your lesson planning and will save you much time at the end. Whether you have fifty-five minute classes or are on a block schedule, your lesson should always flow flawlessly from beginning, middle, and end, with an emphasis on the student work period. Usually, school systems design a grandfather curriculum map as a source of teachers' pacing per grade level and subject area. If there is one available to your district, use that grandfather guide to create your personal pacing guide for your unit to allocate sufficient time to teach and assess students. Although it has been described as a prescribed curriculum, I have always used it to my advantage, and because of it, I was able to provide a snapshot of the content, skills, and activities I was planning to teach. One study finds that teachers can benefit from resources such as pacing guides designed to help them figure out what to teach and how to teach it (Kauffman, Johnson, Kardos, Liu, & Peske, 2002). Keep in mind that some units are larger than others and can take several weeks to complete while others may be shorter. Regardless, utilizing an instructional unit pacing guide similar to the one you see in Figure 13 will assist you in your planning and will give you an overview of the unit and the direction you need to go; it is your roadmap to when you will cover what standards and the time period to cover it. This road map gives an overview of what standards you will cover in a unit per week, what the primary focus will be, what learning activities will ensure that students master the standard, what key terms, and academic vocabulary students need to be familiar with, and which resources will be utilized. Although there are many variations, Figure 14 can aid with structuring your guide. This can also be used as a reference tool to allow you to know which standards students have mastered or which ones need to be retaught; you can keep a record of what and when the standards are taught. Because it takes more time and effort at the forefront, collaborating with

TEACHING METHODS AND STRATEGIES

Unit Instructional Pacing Guide Template Sample

Timeline	Standards to Cover/ Lesson Focus	Focus Question	Activities/ Assignments/	Key Terms for Students to Know	Resources
Week 1	ELAGSE7RL1: Cite several pieces of textual evidence to support analysis of what the text says explicitly as well as inferences drawn from the text.	Why is textual evidence essential to a reader's understanding?	• Jack and the Beanstalk story • ACES strategy • Graphic Organizer	• inference • analyze • explicit/implicit • textual evidence • conclude • justify	• Model: Anchor Chart • Highlighter • Based Term Chart • Article: https://newsela.com/articles/california-native-americans-ocean/id/32384/
Week 2	ELAGSE7RL3: Analyze how particular elements of a story or drama interact (e.g., how settings shape the characters or plot).	How do the story elements interact with one another in the text?	• AR book • Create plot book • Characterization Chart	• Mood • Setting • Symbol • Theme • Conflict	• Characterization, plot diagram, exposition, rising action, climax, falling action, resolution • Three Little Bears Example
Week 3	ELAGSE7RL6: Analyze how an author develops and contrasts the points of view of different characters or narrators in a text.	How do I analyze the differences in how two authors approach the same topic?	• Venn diagram • Rikki Tikki story	• first-person, third-person omniscient, and third-person limited • Objective • Complexity	• Teaching video - www.teachingtube.com • Student video & lesson - www.learnzillion.com

Figure 13

colleagues of similar discipline areas and grade levels will make this process smoother. Your instructional guide will provide an overview of the standards you will teach on a weekly and daily basis to fulfill the curriculum's requirements. Weekly/daily plans should not be ten pages long, although it is not uncommon, but very unnecessary. Organized weekly/daily plans should provide a simple presentation of instruction. Be concerned with student mastery, and don't fall short of providing good instruction by attempting to stay on schedule to adhere to a set calendar. Ultimately, always build in sufficient time in your pacing guide to reteach unmastered standards, skills, and concepts.

No matter how students come to you, you are expected to reach them where they are and take them where they need to be. It is challenging, especially since some students vary in their academic abilities; some are below grade level and in some cases, many grade levels below where they should be. This, with a mixture of English Language Learners (ELL), high achievers, gifted and talented, and average learners in one setting, is a combination that requires planning on purpose. How do you reach each student in a single class? Teach the standards using a backwards design, also known as Understanding by Design (UBD). When planning, one starts with the end—the desired results (goals or standards)—and then derives the curriculum from the evidence of learning (performances) called for by the standard and the teaching needed to equip students to perform (Wiggins and McTighe, 2006). There are three stages to the backwards design that build off each other :

Stage 1: Identify desired results

- What should students know, understand, and be able to do?
- What content is worthy of understanding?

- What enduring understandings and essential questions are desired?

Stage 2: Determine acceptable evidence of learning

- How could you or will you know you've been successful or reached your goal?
- How will you know if students have achieved the desired results?
- What will you accept as evidence of student understanding and proficiency?

Stage 3: Design learning experiences and instruction

- What enabling knowledge (facts, concepts, principles) and skills (processes, procedures, strategies) will students need in order to perform effectively and achieve desired results?
- What will need to be taught and coached, and how should it be taught, in light of performance goals
- What materials and resources are best suited to accomplish your goals? (Wiggins & McTige, 2006)

Using the backwards design can help avoid pitfalls. Time is allocated to reteaching any standards that were not mastered instead of moving on to the next topic of study without all students on board. In Figure 14, a clearer understanding of the backwards design can be compared and contrasted to the traditional planning process.

Traditional Planning Process	Backwards Design Planning Process
Select standards or topic to cover	Select standards or topic to cover
Begins with inputs—develop learning experiences and activities for students to engage in	Begins with outputs—develop an assessment to determine student success for outcome
Teach	Develop learning experiences and activities for students to engage in
Give an assessment (often from a textbook or other resource)	**Teach**
Determine results and give feedback to class and/or students	Assess results using assessment developed in Step 2
Choose new topic to cover	Give feedback
	Reteach or choose new topic

Figure 14 (Newman, 2013)

After you've digested your district's curriculum guide, design your lesson plans. I am a lesson plan advocate. However, I've witnessed some classes without a fully developed plan, and the class, ironically, turned out great, but I always pondered how much more effective the learning environment would have been if more careful planning was done. I have occasionally skipped a lesson plan. I'll also admit that as a seasoned educator, I could go in and give a decent lesson without sitting for hours and having a ten-page lesson plan. But, how much more effective could I have been if I really mapped out and addressed each student's need? Planning a lesson is worth it. It's not only worth just doing it as a requirement, but it's important to do it well. It is as equally important as the aforementioned chapters of incorporating a discipline plan for good classroom management and developing a plan to develop and maintain healthy relationships with students. Having these three organizational tools in place will make your job flow nicely and will keep the learning environment solid.

Lesson planning is the single most important factor of organizing instruction and is the key to effective teaching, although it can be the most difficult part if not properly aligned. Combining standards, objectives, assessments, and assignments that are positioned with the end result in mind are the most important elements of designing powerful lessons; your lesson will flow effortlessly. On the contrary, without effective planning, your end result will not yield the best results. A lesson plan will keep you on track while the students' individual needs are in the forefront. Duplass (2006) suggests that lessons can be planned effectively by asking certain questions that will aid teachers in developing challenging lessons:

1. What goals and standards are important?
2. What background knowledge do students have?
3. How long will it take to teach the lesson and what materials are needed?
4. What big ideas are important?
5. What processes will enhance learning of basic skills of the lesson?
6. How is the lesson relevant to students' lives?
7. What tasks will the students complete?
8. How will the lesson be differentiated to meet the needs of all the students?
9. How will the students change in their thinking because of this lesson plan? (Duplass, 2006).

There is much "behind the scenes" work that has to be put into structuring lesson plans. It is beneficial as a great foundational base to build future lessons off the mastery level of previous lessons. Reflect on the goals, and then adjust the plans accordingly so that all goals are met. Write lesson plans in a way that if there was a substitute or colleague in your class, he or she could carry your lesson for you. With proper planning, the learning environment will reflect your time and effort (Figure 15).

Planning interactive and engaging lessons takes time; it takes years to create your personal library of effective, high engaging activities. But, once you've created the best lessons ever, continue to build and tweak them to meet students' needs. You won't have to recreate the wheel year after year. Just as we require students to reflect on assignments and assessments, the end result of the lesson is your assessment. Reflect on your lesson. This is the only way to improve. What activities were most successful? Did you engage all learners? Did everyone master the standard? How do I determine if students have mastered the standard? How and when will I reteach? What assignments will students who've mastered the standards do next?

If instruction is boring, students will make you aware. Sometimes it is not verbal, but through discipline issues. We have to engage the disengaged and not just ignore them because they are quiet or because it takes too much time. If students have their heads down in your class, that is a problem. Unless there are issues out of your control, if that student who usually has his or her head down continues to do so throughout the year, what will you do to address this? I've been there. One of my students in particular—despite my attempts or threats—would continue to have his head down and be totally tuned out during the lesson. He became my motivation to create better lessons. When I began deliberately planning, I assessed my effectiveness when he began to stay up throughout the class and engage in lessons. I found his currency and used it to hold his interest. He needed little interaction and more autonomy. I provided what he needed. He was

DESIGN QUESTIONS
Stage 1: Identify desired results
Established Goals: • What relevant goals (e.g., content, course or program objectives, student learning) will your design address?
Understandings: • What are the big ideas? • What specific understandings about them are desired? • What misunderstandings are predictable? / Essential Questions: • What provocative questions will foster inquiry, understanding, and transfer of learning?
Students will know . . . • What key knowledge and skills will students acquire as a result of this innovation? • What should they eventually be able to do as a result of such knowledge and skills? / Students will be able to . . .
Stage 2: Determine acceptable evidence
Evidence: • How will students demonstrate the desired understandings? (Strive to identify authentic tasks.)   ∘ By what criteria will student understanding be judged? • Through what other evidence (e.g., quizzes, texts, academic prompts, observations, homework, journals) will students demonstrate achievement of the desired results? • How could students reflect upon and self-assess their learning?
Stage 3: Plan what needs to happen for desired results
Learning Activities: What learning experiences and instruction will enable students to achieve the desired results? How might your design: • Help students know what is expected? • Help you understand students' prior knowledge (or lack thereof) and interests? • Gain and hold student interest? • Equip students to explore the issues and experience key ideas? • Provide opportunities to demonstrate, rethink, and revise their understanding of the course ideas and their work? • Allow students to evaluate their work? • Help you tailor the course to students' different needs, interests, and abilities? • Be organized to maximize engagement and learning?

Figure 15 One-page Template with Design Questions for Teachers

self-directed and needed more of a challenge. My lesson plans from that point on reflected a section for Independent Learners, and I discovered several students in my other classes could benefit from learning this way. During some activities, these students would work with the class as a whole, or with a partner, while other times I would work with them one-on-one to assess their level of understanding by engaging in conversation.

Gone are the days that we allow students to read from a textbook and answer discussion questions at the end of the chapter. Students have to be engaged in lessons. For example, instead of reading about the Solar System, allow students to use themselves as models to recreate it. Instead of just reading about The Diary of Anne Frank, let them access a virtual tour so it becomes more vivid, or allow them to draw the floor plan based on the book's description. When problem solving in math, instead of reading and answering questions, allow students to draw a visual representation of the problem while explaining the steps collaboratively. To make word problems more exciting, include student names in the questions. Students usually get a kick out of reading the problem and stumbling across their name. When teaching Economics, make it relevant by assigning a scenario. Include a different job or career for students and have them research how much they would earn monthly and yearly. Allow them to maintain their standard of living (transportation, food, other expenses) based off their income. Throw a curveball and assign some with families. Use a wide array of strategies to help them learn in a non-traditional way. Although worksheets can be used as a supplement, don't allow that to be the primary activity.

Differentiation Made Easy

One of my biggest challenges as a teacher during my beginning years was differentiating lessons. It was too hard and took too much time. It would be easier to just teach to the middle, then everyone would get a little something. Then, I thought I would differentiate by assigning more work to challenged learners and less work to struggling learners; I was wrong. Some of my students would be disengaged, and I discovered that some of my high achieving, well-disciplined students began having behavior problems. I had to improve my instruction. Tomlinson (2000) states that differentiation means tailoring instruction to meet individual needs. Whether teachers differentiate content, process, products, or the learning environment, the use of ongoing assessment and flexible grouping makes this a successful approach to instruction. Students don't learn in the same way, so how do we teach all students in a single class with various abilities, interests, and motivation levels? Gardner's (1979, 1983) theory of multiple intelligences proposed that people have different cognitive/learning/thinking styles. If every lesson is uniform for all students from beginning to end, it is a disservice to students and to your professional development. We are charged with successfully reaching each and every student during each lesson. If we recognize their individual learning style, create activities based off their interest, and assess their readiness level, then when planning, teachers should vary the content, process, and product. Planning in a meticulous way to address differences will result in an increased motivation to learn. Differentiating will become easier with time as you plan lessons. First, design your lessons based on students' learning style preference. Then, group their shared interests or ability on the lesson. (Keep in mind students may not be strong in every area so this will continue to change). Make sure to formatively assess students (which I talk about in this chapter), and adjust your content to meet your students' need. Use the Student Tracker Chart in Figure 16 to track and document student progress. Conduct an item analysis, the examination of individual items on a test, rather than the test as a whole, for its difficulty, appropriateness, relationship to the rest of the test, etc., so when you reteach you have pinpointed the deficiencies.

Content: What are students learning? How will students access the information? Should all students begin in the same place? If Student 1 knows his multiplication facts, but Student 2 does not, should I teach multiplication facts to both students? Am I maximizing instructional time? Student 1 is getting what he needs but Student 2's time could be put to more use. How can this threaten the learning environment? I must differentiate what the students are learning and adapt what I am teaching (Figure 17). I may elect to assign Student 2 division based on what has already been mastered. Do this by using pre-assessment data to determine readiness. We will hear more about assessing formatively further in this chapter.

How do I differentiate the content when all students in class are reading the same novel? How will students access the information? By modifying it. Struggling readers may listen to the audio version at the learning station, while more advanced learners may read independently. I may also position myself closer to the learning station and at various checkpoints ask questions to monitor their comprehension.

Process: How will students learn the information? After the skill has been introduced and accessed, plan activities that are engaging while matching their ability with the assignment's level of complexity. Activities should be be aligned to address the expected outcome. Students' learning styles and preferences really comes into play. I determined my learning style before any of my teachers

TEACHING METHODS AND STRATEGIES

Class Period:

Assignment:

Standard/Objective Assessed:

Week of:

Mastery	Borderline	Non Mastery	Reteaching Methods #
80-100%	70-79%	69-0	
Student Name(Score)	Student Name(Score)	Student Name(Score)	
Reteaching Methods:			

Reteaching Methods:
1. After School Tutoring
2. Peer Tutoring/Collaboration
3. One-on-one Remediation
4. Additional Time to Complete Task
5. Modeling (*Think Aloud/ Samples/Examples)
6. Graphic Organizers
7. Additional time provided
8. Additional Resources (Online, Video, Manipulative, Visuals)
9. Other

*Think Aloud: modeling the process while explaining your thinking

Figure 16

did. Fortunately, many of my own teachers provided visuals of material they presented, which worked in my favor as a student. If I am given driving directions orally, I would listen and take mental note, however, by the time I attempted to reach my destination, it was guaranteed that I would become lost because I am a visual learner. Even as an adult, while listening to sermons, I draw illustrations and make annotations with various highlighter colors to help my understanding. The material must also be in my hands as I'm following along. In the same way, if students are visual or hands-on learners, add manipulative supports to differentiate the process of learning. Students will also appreciate being able to choose. Provide various options for students to capitalize on their motivation and interests.

Product: How will students demonstrate their understanding of what they now know and are able to do? A written test can provide good insight to a student's level of understanding on a topic or skill; however, what other projects and activities, besides paper and pencil, can teachers use to assess their students' understanding? Students take ownership of their learning when given a choice on how they want to demonstrate their understanding. A good product causes students to rethink what they have learned, apply what they can do, extend their understanding and skill, and become involved in both critical and creative thinking (Tomlinson, 2001). All products should include a rubric.

Grouping Configurations for Instruction

It is important to consider grouping techniques for instructional delivery. Whether you group by individual, whole, or small group, each structure can be successful when implemented purposefully. There is no one solution; how you group is dependent

TEACHING METHODS AND STRATEGIES

DIFFERENTIATION INSTRUCTION		
CONTENT (What are students being taught?)	**PROCESS (How will students learn the content?)**	**PRODUCT (How will students demonstrate what they've learned?)**
• leveled reading • audio/video recorded material • minilessons • CliffsNotes • journal: what do you know about the topic • highlighted text • reading buddies • multi-level questions • modeling • small group instruction	• learning centers/stations • manipulatives • learning menus/choice boards • peer teaching • independent learning • role playing • varied graphic organizers • tiered activities • jigsaw • direct instruction • labs	• design a brochure • perform a skit • give a speech • write a report • make an illustration • create a rap or song • design a web page • conduct a debate • create a game • create a recipe • develop an exhibit

Figure 17

upon the task; therefore, you must distinguish which method is most suitable. The objective + the student task = intended group interaction. Am I introducing a new skill? Are there misconceptions that need addressing in a skill or concept? Are there a few students who haven't grasped the skill or concept? Small groups are impactful to gauge the knowledge of the group. It provides a way to get closer to students. Tomlinson and Imbeau (2010) have noted that teachers can differentiate content, process, and product. Small-group instruction allows teachers to vary the instructional materials they use, the level of prompting or questioning they employ, and the products they expect. Do students have an assigned role? Are they working collaboratively? What activity are they completing? Whole group works well when there is a need to present a topic. Am I introducing a new skill or concept? Is there a class debate or discussion? Additionally, one-on-one provides a way to determine the student's specific needs and directly address any misconceptions. Effective classroom management, as discussed in the previous chapter, is necessary when providing one-on-one or group instruction. As stated previously, if your classroom management is in order, your class—during instruction—will run smoother. Students may take advantage of the opportunity to get off task, so although you may be with one group, continue to keep your eyes on the class with your back never turned away from the masses. Divvy up your time amongst groups and don't spend all your time at one location, but spend no more than four to six minutes rotating around from group to group or person to person. Use your discretion based on their academic needs and the makeup of your class. Address any areas of weakness that need attention. If the student needs more assistance than the time allotted, this is when you must get creative in how you plan on reteaching. This may mean working with them outside of school hours or even conducting a working lunch. This may also mean providing other resources such as videos and web-based resources. However, remember, you are their best teacher.

View the chart in Figure 18 to determine which structure works best when teaching.

> "Frequently vary the delivery of your instruction. Often times we as teachers get caught up in doing things one way. We are as much creatures of habit as anyone. When things become boring and too predictable, discipline problems are undoubtedly going to become an issue."
>
> —Joseph D

Group Structure	Why Use?	Sample Activities
Small Group	• for those making minimal gains • reteaching • to focus on a single skill/concept • to provide greater focus • to provide immediate feedback • limited resources	• Researching • Peer editing • Reteach
Whole Group	• introducing a new skill and concept • providing an overview • lectures • when everyone is doing the same activity • reteaching when the majority may not have an understanding • presenting a class novel • class discussion • direct instruction • modeling	• Viewing a video • Note taking
One on One	• Address specific needs • Determine specific deficiencies	• (Re)teaching skills

Figure 18

Rubrics

I was first introduced to rubrics while in a high school English class. It provided me with structure and a clear understanding to complete my assignment proficiently. Unfortunately, all teachers did not do this which, resulted in a few lower grades on assignments since their expectations were not clear from the beginning. Why weren't other teachers jumping on the bandwagon, because this was certainly helpful? Since then, implementing rubrics has gained necessary momentum in classrooms everywhere. Rubrics are criterion-referenced materials for a task that includes a description, allowing students to measure their performance as they are progressing towards a finished product before it submitting for final review. It should be well constructed with guidelines, but on certain tasks include room for autonomy; this allows students to add their own "stamp." For assignments that are being introduced, provide and review the rubric for students first. The rubric's criteria must match the assignment's intent to clarify the expectation. They provide a way for teachers to provide feedback quickly and easily; students will be able to self-assess and it eliminates anxiety about the expectations. The question of, "How [Why] did I get this grade?" will be clearer to them. Students don't have to figure out what you want from them or hope they are on the right track. There are many free online sources available that allow you to create, modify, or use pre-existing rubrics. Rubrics can be used for any grade level. In primary grades, target your rubrics to meet your students' needs. They may not understand the scale, but include a smiley or sad face to rate their performance. Don't limit rubrics to academics, but use them for lunchroom or hallway behavior as well! See Figure 19 that can be used for primary grades.

LUNCH ROOM BEHAVIOR		
☹	🙂	😁
I did not use my inside voice.	I used my inside voice.	I spoke just above a whisper.
I did not say "please" and "thank you"	I said "please" and "thank you"	I said "please" and "thank you", I chewed with my mouth closed
I left my area dirty.	I cleaned up after myself.	I cleaned after myself and helped my table.

Figure 19

TEACHING METHODS AND STRATEGIES

Use this list of sites to find and create rubrics. Please note: All resources/links were current at time of publication.

- iRubric: create your own rubric or build off the work of other teachers.
  http://www.rcampus.com/indexrubric.cfm
- Rubistar is a free tool to help teachers create quality rubrics.
  http://rubistar.4teachers.org
- TeAchnology: TeAchnology provides free and easy to use resources for teachers dedicated to improving the education of today's generation of students.
  http://www.teach-nology.com/web_tools/rubrics/
- ReadWriteThink provides educators, parents, and after-school professionals with access to the highest quality practices in reading and language arts instruction by offering the very best in free materials.
  http://www.readwritethink.org
- Teacherplanet provides teachers with resources and tools that will make their teaching jobs a little bit easier.
  http://www.teacherplanet.com/rubrics-for-teachers

Quick Note: Early finishers

From time to time, you may have students who finish their work before class has ended. You may not be available to check their assignment, but do not allow students to sit idle. Bored bodies become busybodies. Set up a class station where students can always retrieve extra, fun assignments, whether a handout or online. Assignments can be an assortment of activities from review assignments or introductory work. Choose to assign bonus points for buy-in. Please note: If students are consistently finishing early, evaluate their ability level and your planning. Ask yourself, "Why are students finishing too soon?"

Nine-Week Unit Tracker

What inferences can be made about each student? Which student achieved more? Study the chart in Figure 20 below.

Name	PRETEST	Week 3	Week 6	POST TEST	Mastery?	Growth (+/-)
Student A	34	55	65	72	NO	+ 38
Student B	52	59	60	61	NO	+ 9
Student C	83	84	80	81	YES	-2

Figure 20

The data of this nine-week unit provides a snapshot of students' progress. Mastery is set at 80 percent while non-mastery is considered below 70 percent. Both the pretest and posttest were accurately aligned to reflect the standards. Pretests determine pre-existing knowledge and gives a glimpse into what students should know by the end of the unit. It measures the starting point.

After administering the pretest, two out of three students scored below mastery level. Although Student A did not meet the expectation, there were significant gains on the posttest. Although the student did not meet 80 percent, there was substantial growth. With more intentional planning, the student will continue to progress. This student should be celebrated for their achievement. Let's look at Student B. After a nine-week unit, the student seems stagnate in growth. What did I do to

TEACHING METHODS AND STRATEGIES

modify instruction for this student? Did I reteach unmastered standards during weeks 3 and 6? What did I do for Student A that seemed to work that I didn't do for Student B? Did I formatively assess? How did I use the information to inform, guide, and adjust instruction? Let's look at Student C. This student had already mastered the standard. What did I do differently for this student? Was the student challenged enough? Should this student have been doing the same lesson activities as students A and B? The data from weeks 3 and 6 serve as intervals, or checkpoints to monitor and document growth before getting to the end of the unit. After each checkpoint, did you conference with any student to develop a plan of action detailing what part you will play and what part the student will play to push them towards mastery?

When we have classes, no matter how large or how small, spending time reviewing and utilizing the data to make instructional decisions can be challenging, but in order to get students where they need to be, it takes time much monitoring and planning. Over time, with practice, it will become easier to disintegrate data. You may develop an easier method to track data; work smarter, not harder. Plan to focus on no more than three levels of academic abilities; usually all students will fit into one of them. For example, for each of my classes, based off my current data, I categorized my students as below average, average, or above average. I always felt as if three different levels of activities had to be assigned, and in some cases I did that; however, I began focusing on two levels which I called, "At" and "Above." Students in the "At" category were considered my lower achievers and barely-made-it achievers. My "Above" students were comprised of students who had potential and needed some push, and high achievers. This allowed me to plan while focusing on two abilities. The learning environment may need adjusting based on student performance. Determine if small group instruction, individual instruction, whole class instruction, or one-on-one is useful per lesson and/or activity. Additionally, engage students in charting their own growth and helping them create personal learning goals. This provides them with a clear picture of where they are and where they should be, so they become the captains of their own ship.

Formatively Assessing

Teachers should never wait until the summative assessment and hope all students will pass. In the same way, if I had checked on my car when I first saw the warning signs, I would have had a working car. I bought my first car while away in college. I lived about an hour and a half from home, so I would drive up almost every weekend and ride out everywhere! I saw a few notifications come on the car's dashboard, but I didn't understand exactly what area of my vehicle needed servicing and didn't investigate it either; I ignored all warning signs, thinking it would be fine. I had places to go and people to see and didn't have time to figure out the problem. Besides, the car would still crank up without a problem, and it could still drive, so I was good, I thought. It wasn't until I went to get an emissions test done and didn't pass! What's wrong with my car? Why didn't I pass my emissions inspection? I couldn't get my registration, which resulted in me not being able to drive the car, so I scrambled to get it fixed. Unfortunately, amongst other things, I drove with no oil for so long that my transmission was now ruined! The repair costs were much more valuable than the car's worth, so I had to let the car go. If I would have properly monitored my vehicle, I could have had it diagnosed and treated sooner and would still have my car.

Similarly, formatively assessing is a measuring tool that pinpoints deficiencies and allows teachers to adjust instruction to give necessary feedback and support to students. Students, in return, are able to self-assess their level of understanding with the intent to improve their learning. Formative assessment

- Emphasizes learning outcomes
- Makes goals and standards transparent to students
- Provides clear assessment criteria
- Closes the gap between what students know and desired outcomes
- Provides feedback that is comprehensible, actionable, and relevant
- Provides valuable diagnostic information by generating informative data

(Greenstein, 2010)

There are warnings signs when students don't understand the material we teach; we can't disregard those red flags. If students struggle in classwork and/or with homework assignments, they won't magically do well on assessments. Do the necessary check-ups to determine what students understand before the end of the unit's assessment.

"To say that you have taught when students haven't learned is to say you have sold when no one has bought. But how can you know that students have learned without spending hours correcting tests and papers? ... check students' understanding while you are teaching (not at 10 o'clock at night when you're correcting papers) so you don't move on with unlearned material that can accumulate like a snowball and eventually engulf the student in confusion and despair."

Madeline Hunter

Taking the time to analyze the checkpoint data is imperative for students to progress, because we can so easily leave kids behind, forming an even wider achievement gap. Ask yourself two questions. Would I want to be in my class as a student? Would I want my child to be in my class? Refrain from adding the "ifs"; it is either yes or no.

If there is a shock factor while reviewing data from the summative assessment or end results, such as a project, mid-term or final examination, or writing assessment, we have dropped the ball somewhere. If there is an expectation that the child is going to fail anyway, we are doing students a disservice. If students have not reached mastery, what is being done to target the deficiency? Monitoring, documenting, and addressing student performances is constant. In order to understand what students know, monitor their progress by assessing, assessing, assessing! It occurs consistently—before lessons, during lessons, and after the lessons are taught. Assessing formatively provides critical information that help adjust instruction based on student needs. If there are not significant gains, what interventions are in place for students to get on track? If they are on track, what enrichments are in place to continue their progress? Make note that if a student's pretest results show a low, non-passing mastery level, but he or she made significant gains—although not meeting mastery level—the student is growing academically; don't stop whatever you are doing.

Quick Ways to Formatively Assess

Checking for understanding, as mentioned before, occurs throughout lessons. There are multiple ways to effectively assess students' understanding and allow them to self-assess their understanding as well. Note: When formatively assessing, you want to gauge what students know independently. Limit partner or group activity.

- **Exit Tickets:** When thinking about ways to check for understanding after the day's lesson, the exit ticket is a popular and simple strategy to incorporate for students to reflect on the lesson. Pose the focus question at the beginning of the lesson, making sure to reference it throughout instruction. Then, allow students to answer the question before departure. No grade should be given. This limits pressure on students and provides you with immediate feedback. The information is solely for assessing their thinking. Use the exit tickets to assess their understanding of the day's lesson, if any. This will guide your instruction the following day. Provide ample time. Although posing this question through an online format is easier when looking at the data, and there will be fewer papers to sift through; however, students can also use paper and pen to write their response. After collecting them, you should evaluate the "temperature" of the class while checking for mastery.

- **$1 Summary:** Students are asked to write a summary sentence that answers the "who, what, where, when, why, how" about the topic. Each word is worth $0.05, or no more than 20 words! Use the dollar bill template that can be found on Google to make it more exciting. Note: Squeezing in twenty words is the fun part, but make sure to focus on the content versus the number of words. Focus on students understanding the gist of the topic. The first student to meet the criteria can be rewarded using an incentive list.

- **Emoji:** Allow students to either draw or choose an emoji that best depicts how they grasped the day's lesson. Then ask students to explain why they chose the particular emoji in a few sentences.

- **Observation:** Walk around the classroom with a note pad while observing students as they work. Check for learning by monitoring their discussions and activity progress. Pay close attention to students who seem frustrated and those who mastered the content. Interact with students as necessary.
- **Five Fingers:** This quick check allows students to self-assess how well they understand the material. It also gives immediate feedback on how to structure the next day's lesson based on the student's response. You pose a simple question such as, "If I were to give you a test today, how well do you think you understand the lesson, and could you pass the test?" Students will be prompted to hold up their fingers to range from 1–5. One (I won't pass) to five (I totally understand). For shy students, they may be allowed to write their number down and hand it to you. These ongoing checks can be done throughout the lesson. Have your clipboard in hand to make notes of students who need small group instruction, extra practice, or independent work.
- **Partner Talk:** Pose the lesson's focus question. As students are discussing, walk around the classroom listening, only chiming in to ask a follow-up question or to elaborate, or clear up misconceptions. Really listen to what they are discussing. Are students right on target? Keep a clipboard to make note of anything you want to address with the whole class, and names of students you feel need reteaching. Note: Don't get stuck with a partner, you want to focus on hearing most, if not all partners.
- **The Roads:** Students will self-assess their level of knowledge on a subject. This is good way to gauge students' level of knowledge at the beginning of a lesson and to measure their understanding at the end of a lesson. It's

TEACHING METHODS AND STRATEGIES

also good for students who need some physical activity. Pre-post signs in four corners of your class:
- *Dirt Road:* I have no understanding on this topic! Help me.
- *Paved Road:* I have a little understanding, but definitely need a push!
- *The Highway:* I have a solid understanding, but need a little review.
- *The Interstate:* I totally understand! I can teach this!

Ask students, "Based on your knowledge of (the content taught), which corner best fits your understanding of the lesson? Give students time to think and move. After students stand in their respective corners, allow students to discuss what they know, and choose a group representative to discuss their group's understanding. Rotate to each group as they discuss, without interacting. At the end of the lesson, the goal is for students to not be in the corner in which they started.

Parking Lot: Gather students' questions in a designated section within your classroom [ie., a bulletin board] where students can write any questions about any of the content taught. They can write their question anonymously on a post-it note, or write their name on the back, and place it on the parking lot. Don't allow questions to go unanswered for too long. A week's time is sufficient. Determine if the questions are common, because reteaching may be necessary.

The data you collect from formatively assessing steers instruction. The goal is for all students is to reach mastery; provide them with scaffolded instruction in order for them to be successful. Move away from the traditional paper and pencil quizzes and into more stimulating assessment activities. They can be fun and enjoyable for both teachers and students, and will limit you grading stacks of paper and pencil work. Please note, again, if your classroom management is not up to par, your instructional techniques won't be as effective.

Please note: Some students may be uncomfortable with self-assessing themselves in front of others. Therefore, pose the question online so that they may remain anonymous to the class. Technology has made evaluating the data from formatively assessing easier. Smart boards and websites such as nearpod.com help teachers synchronize lessons across all student devices in the classroom to get real-time feedback and post-session reports on student comprehension. Additionally, websites such as kahoot.com or quiziz.com will allow you to poll students for real-time feedback of student understanding.

*Please note, the resources stated were current at the time of publication.

Why Standards-Based Instruction?

Have your students ever taken a test, and when they finished, they stated that "You didn't teach us this!" It is one of the worst feelings ever; you feel that you dropped the ball. When your lessons, assignments, and assessments aren't aligned, this poses a real threat to students, not only academically, but emotionally. How can this impact the confidence of students if they are assessed on what hasn't been taught? There have been numerous classrooms I have observed where teachers were teaching only what they wanted to teach and not what they were required to teach. It is OK to provide nice-to-know instruction along with what is needed to know; however, focusing on the state/district's requirements is necessary. Learning should be designed around the standards. I've also observed teachers teaching at a lower level.

Keep the level of rigor in the standards high. What am I expected to teach? What activities will equip students with the necessary knowledge to achieve? Have you viewed the state's and district's requirements by grade level? If you are using standards to guide your instruction, you are on target. Standards-based instruction has been around for a while now; however, it always surprises me when teachers are still not using standards to drive their instruction. Some material you may teach is considered nice to know, but make sure you target what students need to know. Check your state's department of education website and/or district website for your grade level and content standards. They do not express how to teach, but what to teach. Then you are empowered with the instructional delivery of the standards; this is the fun part.

Learning Progression

"Learning is not viewed as a series of discrete events, but rather as a trajectory of development over time in a vertical fashion connecting knowledge, concepts, and skills within a domain over multiple grade levels" (Heritage, 2008). When planning lessons, and if your lessons build on each other, it is good practice to review the grade level standards prior to and after your lessons. This will allow you to gather a better of understanding of what students should know and what students need to know before exiting your class for the school year. You will also be able to continue building your toolset of successful resources and materials in order to accomplish student performance goals.

4th grade standard	5th grade standard	6th grade standard
ELAGSE4RL6: **Compare** and **contrast** the point of view from which different stories are narrated, including the difference between *first- and third-person narrations*.	ELAGSE5RL6: **Describe** how a narrator's or speaker's *point of view* influences how events are described.	ELAGSE6RL6: **Explain** how an author develops the *point of view* of the narrator or speaker in a text.

Figure 21

**Please note: ELAGSE4RL6 stands for English Language Arts Georgia Standards of Excellence (Grade) 4 Reading Literature (Standard Number) 6

In brief, Figure 21 provides a view of the same standard domain for three consecutive grade levels; each verb is highlighted to emphasize the standard's progression from 4th-6th grade levels. These standards are building blocks to the next. Before students are able to explain how an author develops the point of view in the 6th grade, the student must have acquired foundational knowledge of different points of view, characterization/traits, narrative voice, and plot in previous grades.

Sixth grade teachers should not spend the school year teaching first-, second-, and third-person point of view; that should have been mastered in the fourth grade; however, if the student has not acquired this, focus on prioritizing the skills needed to move the student toward grade-level standards. This may look like embedding what students should have acquired into their current grade-level content.

Lesson Structure and Progression

The best storytellers capture your attention and hold your interest until the very end. They structure the story coherently while transitioning from the beginning, middle, and end. Similarly, planning a lesson should include the same characteristics. Effective time management takes practice. Some teachers plan lessons but aren't able to get to the core because they can get absorbed in a certain part of the lesson or don't have time to close out lessons because it's time to transition to the next subject. When teachers pace lessons appropriately, it allows the students an opportunity to learn. Transitions should remain smooth and can be aided with a timer or signals. Spending too much time on one part can drag on and become boring to students, on the contrary, moving too quickly can become frustrating if they aren't given time to properly process the information resulting in shutting down. Every lesson should not be treated equally. For a new concept, the pace may be slower than a review lesson, which can move more quickly. The solution is to carefully plan from bell to bell based on the objectives. There should be no dead time in between the beginning, middle, and end of the lesson, which should be prevalent every day. If there aren't enough hand copies or if any learning aids aren't easily accessible, the instructional flow is being compromised. Prepare for smooth transitions and be well prepared each day to avoid unnecessary downtime. Technology will not always be your best friend and work at the press of a button; therefore, plan backups for those "just in case moments" to keep the lesson flowing, regardless.

1. **The Beginning.** At the beginning of all lessons, you, the teacher, are the deliverer of the content. Present clear objectives and goals while keeping the end result in mind. Have I pre-assessed students' knowledge? What

are students expected to know by the end of the class period? How will I make sure students get there? Your goals should be stated throughout the lesson, not just at the beginning, so students will keep in mind the lesson's focus and what they are supposed to know. Posting the standards in student-friendly terms takes away the intimidation factor. If standards are easier to understand, students will understand what they are expected to learn. How well you present the information can capture or lose students' interest.

2. **The Middle.** This is the meat of the lesson where students focus on the task. How are students working? Small groups? Centers? Whole Class? Independently? Learn by doing. Your role is to consistently check for understanding.

3. **The End.** Close out your lesson. It is a lost art. Not because teachers don't know how to close a lesson, but if you don't manage your pacing, it is difficult to give a sufficient closing that authentically assesses students' understanding. Have students mastered the objective? How do you know? Do not let students leave your class with you not knowing if they understood the lesson.

Gradual Release of Responsibility

According to Fisher and Frey, 2007, learning should shift from teacher knowledge to student understanding and application. This shift includes four components, Direct Instruction, Guided Instruction, Collaborative Instruction, and Independent Learning. To sum it up,

TEACHING METHODS AND STRATEGIES

Component	What it Looks Like:
Direct Instruction (I do):	Modeling
Guided Instruction (We do):	Leading students through the task
Collaboration (We do together):	Application/Practicing/Group work
Independent (You do on your own):	Application/demonstrate level of understanding

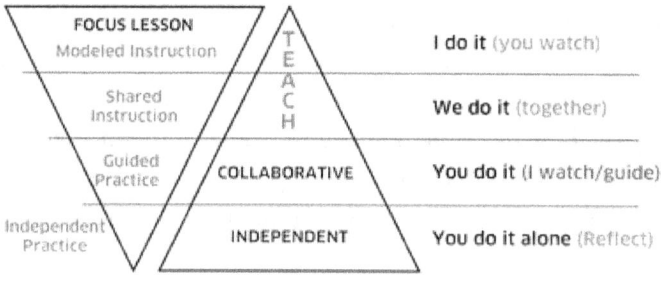

Figure 22 Adapted from Doug Fisher, 2008

During direct instruction the teacher performs a think-aloud, which allows learners to understand the thinking process. Teachers reveal what is going on in their minds by providing clear examples as students observe. Direct Instruction can take minutes or longer depending on the complexity of the skill presented. For students to grasp understanding, go step by step while making necessary connections. Guided instruction means exactly what it says. Teachers guide and students participate. Learning is being transferred from teacher to student. Students may began to feel challenged; therefore chunk information as necessary. This may prompt questions where clear explanations are needed. Throughout guided instruction, be sure to monitor their understanding. As you continue to build healthy relationships with your students, tailoring your techniques to fit their individual needs will become easier to identify. Additionally, students will be more welcoming to you when you work with them one on one or with a small group. Therefore, continue to maintain good relationships with all students.

Fisher and Frey noted, "When done right, collaborative learning is a way for students to consolidate their thinking and understanding. Negotiating with peers, discussing ideas and information, and engaging in inquiry with others gives students the opportunity to use what they have learned during focused and guided instruction." During this phase, students will begin applying what they know together. This allows students to engage in discussion and ask questions. Students are the primary focus on instruction.

The Independent Learning component is essential to the transfer of knowledge. In order for independent learning to occur, students should have gone through all components of the gradual release of responsibility. According to Fisher and Frey (2007), "The effectiveness of independent learning, however, depends on students' readiness to engage in it; too many students are asked to complete independent tasks without having received the focused or guided instruction they need." Their independent learning benefits them now, and it also builds life skills into adulthood. Students begin to take responsibility of their learning, and their motivation and confidence will increase; they will begin to take risks. Students need to become critical thinkers and decision makers. No matter what age group, independent traits should be nurtured and supported.

The gradual release of responsibility model of instruction requires that the teacher shift from assuming "all the responsibility for performing a task ... to a situation in which the students assume all of the responsibility." (Duke & Pearson, 2002)

All in all, don't wait until later in the school year to start the fun, interactive lessons because you want to get their behavior straight first. Start from Day 1. Bring their lives into the classroom and create meaningful and relevant lessons. One mistake teachers make is assuming students won't do well on certain assignments, so we stay away from assigning them. Just as students are encouraged to take risks, you do the same as the instructional leader; take risks with students, the outcome may surprise you.

Your instructional method is not a one-size-fits-all. Have I had non-stellar teacher performance evaluations? Sure! But they only made me a stronger educator. I realized my deficiencies and made it my business to sharpen my craft. I adopted and adapted instructional practices to fit my students' needs. Don't reinvent the wheel. Stay abreast of current trends in education. It seems like every other year, a new study comes out, or one study negates the previous. Know what is going on. Connect yourself with teacher organization groups, attend workshops, and read about what's going on in classes nationally and internationally. Additionally, many districts offer teacher models or academic coaches to support classroom teachers. Take advantage of this. I was fortunate to have a teacher model who demonstrated a lesson for me during a class period. I contacted her during my first year of teaching because I didn't feel as if I was, as I stated, "teaching right," or giving students what they needed. She asked for the standards I was planning to cover. I emailed her, and she took it from there. During her visit, I learned so much. She walked around the class while engaging students; their eyes stayed on her. Her lesson was such high interest that even I would have loved being a student in her class, and although she physically came that one time, how she was able to build an engaging lesson from the standards was invaluable. She sat with me and provided so much support. She encouraged me to give students the learning experience you would want. If it looks boring to you, it'll be boring to them. As I practiced planning instruction, the training wheels came off; I flourished, and the active engagement of my classes was on a high.

Also, search for websites that exhibit exemplary instructional practices and deliveries; search lesson plans for the standards you are teaching to see what and how others are teaching the standards. I appreciated being a faculty advisor for teacher candidates. Not only was I able to provide insight after observing their instruction, but I assessed my own antics and even learned multiple delivery strategies. Don't be an "if only" educator. "If only" I had students who were on grade level... "If only" I taught in a school where we had better technology. Don't let that become your excuse. Gain deeper pedagogical knowledge of your subject area; understand what your content's state and district curricula and standards look like, not just for your grade level, but for the grade levels prior and after yours. This will give you a deeper understanding of what students should already know and what they need to know before exiting the grade level. Locate resources, sign up for professional workshops, contact specific organizations, collaborate with colleagues to stay abreast of current trends and research-based strategies. This will, over time, solidify your toolkit of instructional methods and strategies.

Working Successfully with your Principal

Ultimately, there are two kinds of schools: learning-enriched schools and learning-impoverished schools. I've yet to see a school where the learning curves of the youngsters are off the chart upward while the learning curves of the adults are off the chart downward, or a school where the learning curves of the adults were steep upward and those of the students were not. Teachers and students go hand in hand as learners—or they don't go at all.

(BARTH, R., 2001)

GOOD LEADERS DEVELOP and retain positive outcomes for schools. The principal has great influence on the total climate, culture, and success of the school. Additionally, he or she has significant impact on teacher retention. Principals have the capability to make the working environment challenging and unworkable or pleasurable, trusting, and inviting. However, for success, all parts must work together for the good of the organization. Schools with a high degree of "relational trust" are more likely to make the kind of changes that help raise student achievement. Improvements in such areas as classroom instruction, curriculum, teacher preparation, and professional development have little chance of succeeding without improvements in a school's social climate. (Bryk, A. and Schneider, B., 2002). So what are the effects when a school falls short of a positive working relationship environment? The school will fail. Being a teacher is single-handedly complex. Besides the already challenging day-to-day class environment of lesson planning, assessing, behavioral challenges, and parental involvement (or non-involvement), factor in faculty meetings, content meetings, meeting about meetings, and other appointed meetings; these events can really drain your stamina. Teachers spend the majority of their day in their classroom, so before we go into depth in this chapter, no matter what, make your classroom your sanctuary. You are the ruler of your world, no matter what goes on the outside of your four walls. Create an atmosphere where your class becomes your safe haven. I've run to my empty class, shut the door, turned off the lights, and have had numerous "whoosah" moments. It's the best alternative. It is also good to incorporate your "happy place," whether it be pictures of your loved ones or places you've visited; create your haven.

Some principals and administrators have been teachers at one point or another, too. However, their position is now different. Some leaders will sympathize with you during certain situations, some may take a more political approach when dealing with circumstances, while others are far removed to remember life as a classroom teacher. Either way, continue modeling a positive attitude and stay as upbeat as possible. As my former pastor used to say, "Let no one steal your joy!"

In this chapter, we will dig deep into the most common educational leadership styles, then you will be provided with examples and research-based suggestions on how to be successful while interacting with your school leader. The style of the leader is the way in which he or she uses their authority to lead other people.

Every leader is unique. Although leaders may use a specific style, they rarely use one approach exclusively. It is common to adopt several leadership styles depending on the situation, as it is not a one-size-fits-all; therefore leadership styles depend on the case. Regardless of the various modalities you may encounter in your career, one's leadership type should not solely determine your success, professionally. Are you one to say, "I have no idea what my principal does all day?" Is your principal involved, visible, and interactive? Think about the characteristics of your current school's leader. Think about your former ones. How would you describe their leadership styles and abilities? Please note: Principals or headmasters are the instructional leaders, so when discussing leadership, we are focusing on the person who holds this position.

Authoritative Leadership

Under this leadership style, also known as autocratic, the principal prefers to have direct control over all decision making. He or she uses his or her own thoughts, ideas, and judgements regarding policies and procedures of the school. This leader does not consult with subordinates before a decision is made; however the principal expects the decision to be promptly implemented without rebuttals. Good relationships may be more difficult to form since their is no autonomy for staff. There is a lack of initiation and hinderance in communication with staff. Following the "orders" may be looked upon negatively by staff; however, another perspective about this leader is they have clear vision and expectations about what they want and are very self-confident in their abilities. This principal, called the change catalyst, is highly structured.

Example: Donald Trump is considered to have led in this style. Known as one of the wealthiest people in the world, before becoming president, he owned several businesses. His top-down approach made him known for his dictatorship and being in control of decisions. As a result of these characteristics, his businesses have been successful for decades. He is considered highly goal oriented and confident. He's very clear on commanding what should be done, when it should be done, how it should be done. However, some see this as aggressive and straightforward.

How to shine: If you have a good idea that you know will benefit the school, it may be better to keep it to yourself. Also, never take the decisions of the autocratic leader personally. When dealing with this leader, it is OK to adopt the, "it's you, not me" concept. Because the objectives are predetermined by the leader, focus on doing your job well! Focus on obtaining results. How you reached the objectives can be kept to yourself since the autocratic leader is more interested in the destination rather than the journey. Additionally, choose your battles carefully; it is recommended to stay professional at all times without becoming combative or defensive.

Democratic Leadership

Also known as a participative leader, this style is considered most effective of all leadership styles. Tasks are delegated, staff input is encouraged, and workable goals are collaboratively formed. Under this leadership style, there is higher productivity and staff efficacy because there is autonomy and the staff feels valued. The principal welcomes creativity and is open-minded to ideas and questions, and although opinions are solicited, he or she, after considering all ideas, makes the final decision.

Example: Steve Jobs (1955-2011), billionaire and co-founder of Apple Computers, once stated in the *All Things Digital: D8 Conference in 2010*, "If you want to hire great people and have them stay working for you, you have to let them make a lot of decisions and you have to be run by ideas and not hierarchy; the best ideas have to win or otherwise good people don't stay." His business was organized where everyone had a division to oversee. They met for hours once a week where they discussed the business and what daily goals were made to reach the vision. He encouraged teamwork at the top, and that spread throughout the company. Teamwork was built through trust without micro-managing. This has reeled in much success to Apple Computers, even after his death.

How to shine: Communication is open and encouraged; however, before inputting your ideas, make sure to add some expertise before adding your contribution. Back it up with research, statistics, and other data, and be able to clearly articulate how your suggestion will accommodate and improve the organization's vision.

Transformational Leadership

This leadership style initiates change while identifying the need and creating and inspiring the vision. They are considered highly inspirational and change catalysts who empower their subordinates. The strengths and weaknesses of the team are taken into consideration when assigning tasks/duties. Staff are coached and enabled to problem-solve. The vision is linked to daily goals, and all are encouraged to push themselves beyond the limit. Under this leadership, subordinates have high job satisfaction, trust-based relationships are formed, and buy-in is high.

Example: Civil Rights activist Martin Luther King Jr. was known to display this leadership style throughout his fight for equality. He was about building togetherness among people. MLK had a vision and worked at it for others to understand and support his objectives. He elevated his followers to high expectations that may have typically be considered not possible. His vision was transparent as he used his words, actions, and influence to motivate. He was well respected and trusted. He became the example he expected others to be.

How to Shine: Contribute to your school by being involved with committees. Seek out ongoing learning opportunities to improve your instructional practices. Share ideas and talents with colleagues. Join the school improvement committee to add your insight and suggestions. Also, connect yourself with educational organizations and committees within and outside the school district.

Affiliative Leadership

This leadership style is focused on building a sense of belonging and togetherness, which will bring on a sense of loyalty. Trusting relationships among staff, and staff and principal are considered necessary to thrive. The expectation when using this style is to improve morale, mend broken trust, and create a harmonic atmosphere. This leader believes in staff coming first and keeping them happy. This leader gives frequent feedback to ensure everyone stays on target. On the other hand, the leader may be so busy with the emotional aspect of workers that they may overlook poor job performance. They may also have difficulties when staff conflicts arrive. All in all, employees are highly valued.

Many middle school and elementary school teachers are more adjusted in this style because they operate on teams while high school teachers do not operate on the team structure. Make the adjustment as necessary.

Example: Around my sixth year of teaching, my school had a change of principals. There was a lot of turbulence among staff for various reasons. One reason was that after the new principal had taken the position, he made some immediate changes that did not sit well with some, so he sought to build the morale. He really focused on building trust, communication, and a sense of community, which he did successfully. However, while doing a good job focusing on team building and praise, he compromised the assurance that good instruction was occurring. Mediocrity was at its best. Effective strategies weren't being implemented and there was a lack of effort.

How to Shine: Don't settle for mediocrity! Continue to monitor student achievement for growth. Give your students all you've got. We've all heard the phrase "teamwork makes the dream work." Be a team player. When colleagues aren't having the best day, be an encourager. Adopt the phrase, "one band, one sound." Collaborate with your colleagues without being an information hog. Form and lead a committee with the purpose of building the work culture. For example, you can facilitate some "getting along together" activities, or outside of school, you can put together a staff bowling night. When working directly with the principal, although relationships are important to him or her, make sure to distinguish between professional and personal. Discussing private occurrences in our lives should stay private. Mixing business with pleasure is not recommended, although it can be so easy since there is a strong sense of trust. Respect boundaries.

Transactional Leadership

This leadership style allows leaders to achieve their goals based on a reward-penalty system. When in compliance, subordinates are extrinsically rewarded; however, when the leader's orders are not followed, punishment pursues. This leader will not make much effort to ask for input; he or she facilitates clear and concise expectations that are to be met in a timely matter. The reward system is conditional if subordinates meet the objective(s), efficiently. Be aware, if there is a lack of performance, disciplinary action may occur that can form a "paper trail," which can eventually lead to termination. This leader believes in supervision in order for goal achievement.

Example: Athletic coaches are commonly known as transactional leaders. If you play well, you are rewarded, reflecting on the coaches' abilities. If you don't, you may be benched or required to sit out a game.

How to Shine: Be careful not to rely solely on rewards; they can become the motivation, the distraction, the manipulation. Many subordinates may begin to do the minimum requirement to meet goals, which stunts your professional growth. Do more than the minimum, go above and beyond the call of duty. Your goal is always your students' success!

In a perfect world, we would love all of our bosses and be excited to return back to work daily. But in the real world, there will forever be obstacles, dissatisfactions, and challenges that we face. If your working environment is not pleasurable, consider your options. There are a wide range of reasons why teachers seek other working locations when it comes to their administrators. Reasons range from: they don't like the direction in which the school is going; they feel unsupported, whether it is with other colleagues, students, or parental behaviors; they feel bullied; or they feel that no professional growth is taking place. I have never met a teacher who urgently wanted to leave a school where they felt good about their leaders. There was a teacher who even commuted over an hour every day and didn't mind because she loved her school, administration and all. Just as your school leader may have various leadership styles, there will be a mix of leadership styles among other leaders within your building. It is important to quickly learn how they operate in this regard and adapt accordingly so that you are successful in your relationships with them. Just as we teach students to be successful no matter what the circumstance, we should adopt a similar stance with all personnel, whether they are a board member or even a parent.

One particularly colleague I worked with despised the school where she was assigned. Her argument was that she didn't feel supported by administration. I didn't understand. When she first arrived, she was team admin, so what happened? I investigated the root problem: support. Was there a misinterpretation of what support looked like? Administrators, on the other hand, felt that they were very supportive, so was someone right and the other wrong? What does it mean to be supported? Will the principal back you when an aggravated parent believes a class procedure should be changed? Are there staff acknowledgement efforts throughout the school year? Are ideas and staff input encouraged? Are administrators approachable when there is a concern? Is student discipline dealt with, or does it fall back on you? Are professional learning opportunities punitive or used for enhancement? The truth is, support can be very subjective. There can be discrepancies in perspectives. For example, let's look at a teacher who writes numerous discipline referrals and believes that students are not receiving deserving consequences, if any at all. Administrators may look at the discipline reports and feel the referrals are a classroom management problem and should be addressed with the teacher's own classroom discipline plan. Administration may see many disciplinary referrals as a weakness and set up a conference addressing their concern, or may sign the teacher up for classroom management courses. The teacher may feel unsupported while the principal may see things differently. In this case, gathering a better understanding of their expectations is important. To remedy this, I would seek a clear understanding as to what was deserving of a teacher consequence and what would be honored as an office referral. This is similar to what we discussed in Chapter 3. Ask questions to avoid misunderstandings, and have your matrix ready to categorize offenses. Sometimes, all it takes is clarification. But in this case, if there are numerous referrals being written, it may very well be a teacher issue.

It is true that when leaders empower, respect, and value their employees, they will find loyalty. What can you do to support your leader? Try to develop a powerful bond with them, initially.

Ask yourself, What am I doing to better my workplace? What organizations do I lead? How am I contributing to the school's vision? Could I be doing more? Make meaningful moves and be sure to not waste your work! How you see your role in your job is vital to your performance. Your position is important, therefore give it all you've got! It is encouraged to invite administration into your class when you have a great lesson you are excited about and want them to witness. I've done that a few times; however, you won't always have to broadcast what you're doing in the classroom, the shine will come naturally. How can you advance the school's vision and mission? When you shine, so does your school, and principals love that.

Be careful what you say out loud. Everyone is entitled to their own opinion, but know when and if it is safe to solicit it. Watch your mouth; your words become your feelings. It sounds easier than it really is, since it's so easy to join in and become a griper. Stay isolated from the masses. I could say a million Amen's to some of the complaints—or rather truths—from my colleagues because some were completely verified, and to be honest, I joined in at times. Learn from my mistakes. Don't do it. It adds fuel to your fire and will make the workplace even more unenjoyable. Situations won't change because you think they need to, so stay positive. What's even worse is that your name could get in the mix of the "drama club"; you never know who's around. Negativity is so contagious, so surround yourself with positivity. The truth is, any unfavorable situation could interfere with the flow of your classroom. Just as discussed in the previous chapter, emotions drive our attention; teachers are not excluded from this. Feelings, the physical and mental response to emotion, are what can hamper or promote attention (Weiss, 2000).

Some leaders are fueled off of power and egos, and not priority. Not your business. Put yourself on cruise control, and if you feel that you need to make your exit, don't talk about it to others, just do it in a respectable way. The most important role of the principal is that as the instructional leader. He or she guides the professional growth of the staff; we may not understand every decision, but it is necessary to understand that you may not have all the deets on why a decision is made. Just accept it, and move on.

I can't stress enough how vital it is to stay positive, and negative comments should cease. I have discovered staff and administrators who were close, and many weren't aware of the friendships. You never know who's close to who, so be wise and keep your negativity to yourself. I once worked with a teacher who went to an interview with another school and badmouthed his current principal. In all fairness, he wasn't lying in what he said; it was so true, but it was common sense not to do it. Terrible move. To his surprise, everything he said got back to the principal, and he was blackballed from the transfer he so wanted. He ended up having to leave the district. Even if your current situation is unpleasant, no prospected employer wants to hear the gripes of your current situation, and ironically, you will be the one who looks bad. You will be called out for very poor judgment. Unfortunately, from that point on he had difficulties with reaching the expectations of his job requirements and was relieved when the year ended so he could leave the district.

Avoid cliques. It's amazing how adults can be cliquish in the workplace; I experienced it firsthand. As a teen, if anyone would have told me adults were more cliquish in the workplace than teens, I probably would have never believed them. Don't be a loner, but stay out of cliques. Don't be like the movie "Mean Girls." It's almost inevitable to want to be accepted and fit in, yes, even as an adult. Everyone wants to belong. No matter who we are, we all have the same needs: survival, belonging, power, freedom, and fun (Glasser, 1998). Make alliances with everyone, but be as exclusive as possible without being an outsider. Cliques can look a certain way to administrators. You don't want to be known as the troublemaking group, or the difficult group, or to other teachers as the principal's snitch. Remember, when administration is in their office with the door closed, you will be with the "general population." Don't fail to open yourself up to a positive colleague who thinks like you. They can be your strongest support network. Therefore, purposefully set your mind to be friends or kind acquaintances with everyone, but avoid conversations that may cause conflict with others. Keep in mind that you have to work there daily, and having a peaceful working environment is a necessity. With all the other factors you have to deal with, being in opposition with colleagues should not be on the menu.

Learn your administrators' characteristics. Recognize their likes and dislikes. As discussed previously, some principals appreciate straightforwardness while others are not so receptive of accepting ideas that are opposite from theirs. Draw your own conclusion about an administrator rather than drawing on the perceptions and occurrences of others. I had heard horror stories about a few of my principals; fortunately, I never experienced or witnessed it firsthand. Just as teachers have different relationships with their students, so does your boss have different relationships with staff. Rely on your experiences only, not the experiences of others.

There is great value in building a relationship with your principal; these relationships are the heart of the school. Whether you realize it or not, you need their support as much as they need yours. To increase your impact, here are some suggestions:

1. Seek professional development opportunities. Demonstrate your willingness to enhance your practice and polish your craft. Share any resources you may collect with colleagues.
2. Volunteer: The basketball team may need someone to work the scoreboard, a teacher may be needed to teach Saturday school, a committee may need to be led to form assemblies. Make yourself available and be seen outside of the classroom. Do more than the minimum 8 to 4. Going above and beyond is what great teachers do.
3. Stay positive: As the saying goes, "Your attitude determines your altitude. Fight through the negativity, and stay away from the negativity—even if you agree. Principals want their employees at their best. That is when the impact is the greatest. No matter the situation, don't let anyone or anything steal your joy! Be friendly and put on a smile.
4. Be a problem-solver: Remember, if you aren't part of the solution, you're part of the problem. If you come with a problem, provide at least two to three solutions. There is a line between complainers and problem solvers. Complainers are viewed as a Negative Nancy, while problem-solvers seek for ways to improve them.

5. Be Ethical: Follow requests. Arrive on time to work. Come to work. Participate in meeting discussions. Do what is required even when no one is looking.
6. Request an informal observation: Let them see you in action. Show your desire in improving your instruction by inviting the principal to your class for feedback.
7. Get along with others: This includes colleagues and students. The principal is already putting out fires throughout the day and would rather not be involved in conflicts among staff and/or students. Fewer office referrals show that you have good classroom management.
8. Build a positive rapport with parents: Principals would rather do without parent-teacher conflicts, therefore form a partnership by connecting with them. Work well with them. Keep an open mind, and remember, just as we may call our mobile phone companies in concern for a high bill, we expect courteous customer support. We will talk more about this in the next chapter.
9. Be a teacher leader: The truth is, principals can't do it all alone. You are needed. Be a mentor to a new teacher so they can be well adjusted. Go to a workshop and present the ideas to a group. Facilitate an in-service workshop that can benefit colleagues.
10. Put students first: They are the reason you have a job, right? When making a suggestion, you should make sure that you are selfless and keep them in the forefront. Be fair to students. When you have a genuine care and connection with students, everyone will take notice. If a student is failing or doesn't understand a concept, don't accept it. Plan to have a tutorial session with those who need extra help before or after school.

Just as you have a tough job to do, principals have it even tougher. They are responsible for every component of the school including the nutrition department, custodians, parents, all staff, and every student, to name a few. They have myriad things to deal with on a daily basis. You may not understand why things are run the way they are or why certain decisions are made. Just keep in mind that administrators have background information that is not always public knowledge. There may be district mandates and state policies to take into consideration. Don't assume they have bad intentions. The requirements of their position can be tedious, so insert your suggestions only when you have all the background information and, even then, insert them when they are invited. As a professional and an employee, you are obligated to adhere to the leader's guidelines. Whether you like them or not doesn't matter. Respect the rules just as we expect our students to do. Don't loose your purpose under the jungle. Our kids need you. You are appreciated and you are most needed. Don't burn yourself out. When a positive school culture exists between staff and leader, productivity increases.

Building the Bridge to Parental Engagement

One band, one sound

—DRUMLINE

A RE YOU A first-generation college student? Second-generation college student? Or do you come from a family that has many alphabets after your name, eg., MBA, Ed.D., RN, Ph.D., Ed.S? First-generation students are those who are the first to graduate from college in their family. For second-generation students, one or both parents graduated from college. I'm a third-generation college student. Growing up in my household, college was discussed often and was the expectation after graduation. With a grandmother with a Ph.D., who was a principal, a mother who was a teacher, and a dad with an Associates degree from an engineering technology school, and a host of other educators and professionals in my family, higher learning was inevitable to escape. As early as elementary school, I can recall playing school using discarded textbooks and teacher's edition books that I stored on my book shelf in my room to teach my imaginary students. I would reteach what had been taught in school that day—every subject was covered. I would even have a paddle to spank the students who weren't paying attention or causing disruption. (It would usually be "friends" I didn't like in my class; it became a needed daily outlet.) Reteaching to my students was fun for me. During spring and summer breaks, my family would take trips often. We traveled to different states and countries. We carpooled, rented Winnebagos, and took cruises. My mom and grandmother would take my sisters and I to the library weekly to check out books to read. My mom would take my sisters and me to Blockbuster, a popular video store during that time, to find movies to match the books we had just finished reading. My parents would hold writing contests at home where my sisters and I would write books and illustrate them. (I, the youngest child, was always the winner—just to put that out there).

Much family time was spent together. We would have a home-cooked meal while sitting at the dinner table as a family, share how our day went, and discuss current news and happenings with each other almost every day. My parents were involved in my overall schooling and made me understand why education was significant to my life. Homework, class assignments, teachers, and my social relationships (although I wished they would stay out of this) were first, alongside family and God.

Unfortunately, most households and family dynamics of the students I've taught have not mirrored mine. The home environment, from the time the child is an infant to high school age and beyond, is pivotal to a child's academic success. Parents are their child's first teacher, and how they feel about education will be transferred to their child, usually. But what happens when mom and dad aren't present because they have to work late to put food on the table and clothes on their child's back? Or when grandparents or great-grandparents are raising their grandchild because the parent is absent? Or home life is unsafe and unstable? How does this disrupt the flow of school life? There is an achievement gap between low-income and affluent households. What are the roots of the gap, and what role do home and school play in making the gap narrow in hopes of closing it? The National Center for Education Statistics, NCES, (2015), states an achievement gap occurs when one group of students (such as students grouped by race/ethnicity or gender) outperforms another group, and the difference in average scores for the two groups is statistically significant (that is, larger than the margin of error).

A controversial book, The Bell Curve, which was published in 1994 by psychologist Richard J. Herrnstein and political scientist Charles Murray, suggested the achievement gap was inherited. According to them, it was the result of "genetic makeup and natural ability." However, this theory was widely discredited, and experts stated that the widened gaps can be blamed on opportunity gaps and environmental factors. Although as a child I was well traveled and had a strong foundational unit, most students in the inner city do not have these same opportunities to travel, to have deep conversations at home with family, to live in a safe, warming environment, and to sharpen their reading and writing skills with the support of home. Growing up in low-income homes can certainly bring deficits that spill over to school life. There may be a lack of education resources at home, which will reflect at school. Other side effects that support the achievement gap of low-income homes are a deficiency of health care and nutrition. Children in poverty whose parents provide engaging learning environments at home do not start school with the same academic readiness gaps seen among poor children generally (U.S. Department of Education, 2000; Viadero, 2000, Sparks, 2011). Some students enter elementary school without being able to recognize their alphabets, spell their name, or count to 10. According to BookSpring.com,

- Children from low-income families are at greater risk for entering school unprepared. According to a national longitudinal analysis by the U.S. Department of Health and Human Services (HHS), economically disadvantaged children may know only one or two letters of the alphabet when entering kindergarten, while children in the middle class will know all 26. Lee, V. E. & Burkam, D. T. (2002).

- By the age of two, children who are read to, regularly display greater language comprehension, larger vocabularies, and higher cognitive skills than their peers. J., Tarullo, L.B., Raikes, H.A., Rodriguez, E. (2006).
- Children growing up in homes with at least twenty books get three years more schooling than children from bookless homes, independent of their parents' education, occupation, and class. (Evans, M. D., Kelley, J., Sikora, J., & Treiman, D. J. (2010)

According to Start Early, Finish Strong: How to Help Every Child Become a Reader (1999),

> An average child growing up in a low-income family receiving welfare hears one-half to one-third as many spoken words as children in more affluent households. At these rates the low-income child would know about 3,000 words by age 6, while the child of the high-income family would have a vocabulary of 20,000 words. To provide the low-income child with weekly language experience equal to that of a child from a middle-income family, it would require 41 hours per week of out-of-home word exposure as rich as those heard by the most affluent children.

Research has proven that the collaboration between home and school produces a positive, dynamic outcome regardless of socioeconomic status, family education level, or background.

There is a widespread belief that parents, especially of the inner city, are disengaged and devalue education. There have been conflicting views as to why students don't achieve to their maximum abilities. Parents have placed the blame on schools, and in return schools have blamed parents for not being involved in their child's education. Studies have shown that students whose parents are involved in their education are more likely to have positive outcomes such as graduating, having good attendance, and earning higher grades. PI [parental involvement] includes communication with educators, volunteering at schools, fostering learning at home, engaging in the decision-making process at the campus or district level, and participating in school and community partnerships (Epstein, 2002).

It is a fact that some parents fall short of being directly involved with the school, whether in a high-income or low-income area. They aren't as active in their child's education as we would like or from what we perceive. If not for a special school ceremony, a school performance, the taking of an electronic device by a staff member, or the attempted kicking of the teacher's butt because a parent didn't like how one treated their child, we may not ever see a student's parent(s) in the school the entire time the student may attend that school, from months to even years! Despite this, we can't assume that families in lower-income communities don't want the best for their children. Especially as educators, we must avoid deficit thinking—the practice of holding lower expectations for students with socioeconomic, racial, and ethnic backgrounds that do not fit the traditional context of the school system. In fact, parents do have the desire to support their child but don't know the ways to go about doing it. The threat of negative assumptions about families in these demographics hinders schools from providing the best services to students and families in the community. Recently, Rice Univeristy's Kinder Institute for Urban Research conducted a 2013 Houston Education Survey, where it was found that 92 percent of all parents with school-aged children (regardless of ethnicity) said they hoped their child will be able, at a minimum, to graduate from college. There are barriers that have been noted by researchers as to why there are hindrances in parent relationships with school. Some of the reasons have been noted as parents not having the best experiences during their time as a student, and the negative associations keep them away. Researchers have also noted some parents may be uneducated, a middle or high school drop-out, and shy away from being too engaged by attending parent teacher conferences, PTA meetings, and other functions where a discussion of their child's performance may occur; They are unable to help with homework, class assignments and projects and stay away because of inferiority. Standards are more complex than ever before. As the curriculum becomes more advanced, many parents feel less able to assist with their children's homework (Hill & Tyson, 2009). Additionally, with the nation's demographics changing, there are language barriers that keep parents away. Also, there are parents who have various work schedules in order to provide for their family. They sleep during the day while the child is at school and work at night where the child comes home to a parentless environment. Children become the caregiver or are looked after by older siblings. All of these complex situations impact the child's academics; however, we cannot allow these reasons to be excuses as to why we don't expect a child to perform at their best while in our classes.

    Teachers can either build or break the relationship between home and school. Let's focus on your students and parents. What have you done (not the school primarily) past or present, to build the bridge to encourage parental involvement in your class that has been effective? List them.

_____

_____

_____

_____

_____

_____

After reviewing your list, which actions were successful? Unsuccessful? How can you encourage more consistent parental involvement? You, the teacher, have to be the driver and make the initiation to build the bond and stay in contact. It will work in your favor as the school year progresses. Communicating with parents occurs through phone, email, blogs, and class websites; however, after using the questionnaire in Chapter 2, you will be able to identify the homes of students who may not have internet access, therefore find alternative ways to communicate. The first step to build the bridge with home is to make contact with home within the first two weeks of school. (I would not recommend contacting them before then since rosters may change.) You are taking a proactive approach rather than a reactive approach. You want to begin building rapport and a trusting relationship with parents, and begin setting the stage immediately. Middle and high school teachers have more students, so contacting 100 parents is possible, but highly unlikely; however, send a personal letter using the same format or an email blast. Since elementary teachers generally have fewer classes, contacting all parents by phone may be more realistic. Always request current contact information even if it is in the school's database so that parents will be aware of the happenings in your class. Writing a short script may be helpful when calling or emailing. Introduce yourself by stating who you are and what they can expect from this school year such as exciting projects, upcoming field trips, and interactive lessons. This is separate from your course syllabus, it should be more personal. An email or phone call may go as follows:

> "Good morning, may I speak to the parent of Jane Doe?—My name is Ms. Smith from Candy Cane Middle School and I am Jane's new Math teacher. Is this a good time to speak with you? I will be very brief. (If so, continue. If not, set up a time that fits the parent's schedule). I am contacting you because I wanted to personally introduce myself and to welcome both of you to my class! I am so excited for this school year; there will be plenty of projects, engaging and interactive lessons, and plans to attend a few field trips. In the next few days, please look out for items such as the class syllabus, locker and clinic forms that you will be receiving. Please feel free to reach out to me at any time so we can work together to ensure Jane's success!

Usually within the first two weeks of school you will be able to recognize potential problem students; those are the parents you want to be sure to personally contact. Speak nothing negative, just introduce yourself and make a good first impression. You will need their support and cooperation as the year progresses. The phone call should end with the parent understanding you are there for the best interest of their child. Additionally, choose wisely the time of day in which you call. I generally would call parents in the morning or during the day, and I avoided evenings since some parents worked afternoons/evenings while others were getting situated from work. Also, if I needed to call for an important reason and the parent didn't answer, I could leave a message with hopes of them contacting me back the same day. Fortunately, email has made communication more efficient.

Keeping Records

What parent wants to hear negative reports about their child? Contacting parents about deficiencies in behavior and/or academics can be difficult because their response may be uncertain. Some parents may be supportive while others may side with their child. Reactions are uncertain; all in all, making contact is necessary and imperative for their sake and yours. Don't shy away from this. However, keep parents informed but avoid being petty. There is no need to call every single time the student does something wrong. Some things should be handled in-house. If this happens, the parent will deflect from their child's deficiencies and began to blame you, especially if you are the only teacher that contacts them too much. Keep a communication log that may be accessible to other teachers of the student. If one student has multiple teachers, keep an electronic communication log (name, purpose of call, and a one-to-two-sentence summary of the discussion that all teachers can access. The last thing a teacher wants to do is call a parent/guardian with a negative report immediately after another teacher has made a similar call. If there are numerous issues arising from multiple classes, make the call together. Then plan for an in-person conference as a team.

The Overly-Involved and/or Demanding Parent

Although we champion the involved parent, too much contact can become exasperating for you (and the student). Because you are teaching their child, they have a right to check up on them and request any information pertaining to their student. This is part of the job description; however, don't ever feel bullied or harassed. Are the parent-initiated contacts warranted? Are their requests reasonable? If you are becoming overwhelmed with that persistent parent, there are tips to curtail their behavior.

If a parent requests weekly or even a daily progress update, try setting up a communication schedule that works for you, generally every other week or once every three weeks, where you can check in with the parent. If a parent persists to speak more often, just assure them that if you observe the student's behavior or academics need to be "checked" immediately, you will be sure to contact them beforehand. As much as you may (or may not want to), it is not feasible to focus all your attention on one student.

Additionally, does the student have an administration behavior plan? Is the student in a special education or gifted program? Get them involved. Request that they set up an electronic progress monitoring system that is easy for you to complete such as a Google Form. This is sure to keep this helicopter parent in the loop without driving you crazy.

The Unresponsive/Absent Parent

We can't do it all. I'm preaching to the choir when I say that more parents should be involved in their child's education. This would be the ultimate dream, but it doesn't always happen, and it is not always easy. It can become frustrating to try reaching a parent to speak about their child's progress but to no avail, whether academic, behavioral, or both. The connection between home and school is weak and no ally can be formed, yet! Unfortunately, it happens. I once had a parent who never responded to any of my phone calls; she knew the school's phone numbers and would never respond to a voicemail message or a letter mailed to her home. When I attempted to reach her from my own Google phone number, she answered once, and when she discovered it was a teacher from her child's school, she never answered the phone again. Never take this personally, and don't jump to conclusions and think the parent doesn't care. There can be numerous factors impacting the parent's involvement.

After researching student records, I found that the student's parent had been contacted countless times; she was probably sick and tired of hearing about her child. There was negative report after negative report. Were the calls justified? Absolutely! But beating a dead horse does nothing to change the behavior; although there is no formula to make the parent cooperate, there are ways to prompt involvement.

Additionally, watch how often you call a parent about a negative situation. Calling a parent after each incident their child is involved in may not get you their support, and don't be shocked if after a while, your calls go unanswered or they simply tell you to stop calling.

If calling the parent doesn't work, try leaving a voicemail. (Hopefully, you have already made contact with the parent within the first two weeks of school, as discussed earlier, so the parent is at least familiar with you. If you haven't, hope is not lost). When leaving a voicemail, don't let it be about anything negative. Be proactive and just state that it's a routine call that you make for all students around this time of the year, and ask how you can better service their child. Whether it be providing tutorial services after school or in the morning or wanting to schedule a field trip with the class, make sure the voicemail stays in a positive tone.

Attempt to identify why the parent isn't involved, as this may be the key to unlocking the barrier. Could it be a language barrier? Negative personal experiences as a student? Other priorities, such as caring for a sick family member or working several jobs? Therefore, discover ways to engage parents. All in all, don't give up on the parent; use your wit and your desire to connect with them to drive your tenacity. Most importantly, keep documentation of your attempts.

Those Negative Phone Calls We Like to Avoid

Sometimes, certain behaviors do not warrant an email but a phone call. Making negative phone calls home about students can be uncomfortable. You don't know how the parent may respond to what you're saying or the outcome. However, you want to make sure you make contact to keep them abreast of what is occurring, for your sake as well. Whether it is calling because a student has been consistently misbehaving, falling asleep, or fighting, make sure you keep them in the know. Documentation, or keeping records, as stated previously, is everything, and you never know when your records will be beneficial. When calling parents, a huge mistake teachers make is going right for the jugular! They state immediately what the student did wrong. You will be more open to resistance starting off so strongly. It's almost like waking up in the morning. Instead getting out of bed abruptly (like I have had to do when I oversleep and feel discombobulated for half of the day), I have to look at the ceiling for a moment and lie there for a minute or two before stretching and easing myself out of bed. In the same way, you have to start the conversation smoothly before turbulence sets in.

1. State who you are and in general why you are calling (about behavior, academics, or both).
2. Ask if it is a good time to talk. If so, proceed. If not, ask when would be a better time, or have the parent contact you at their earliest convenience.
3. State something positive about the student.
4. Ease into the negative and provide evidence/example of the problem.
5. Show genuine concern and what you hope will change.
6. Ask the parent for their assistance to ensure their child is successful.

7. Update parents with a report. Whether the child has improved or not, the parents need to know. If they haven't improved, plan the next steps. If they improved slightly, praise that slight improvement and encourage them to progress even more.

Example: "Hello, this is Ms. Smith; may I speak to (parent's name)? I'm (student's name) math teacher. I am calling you because I'm concerned about (student's name) recent behavior in my class. Is this a good time to talk? He started the year off very well with no major problems. He was participating, completing assignments and homework; however, I have noticed a change in his behavior where he is starting to become defiant, and he is not completing his assignments, which is beginning to affect his grade. Today in class, he (provide an example of the defiant behavior). I wanted to contact you now because I don't want the behavior to get worse. He is distracting not only himself from learning but others in the class. I have (provide strategy you have used such as had a conference with student, moved the seating), but it is not working as expected. Are you noticing any changes at home?

I will keep in contact with you because I really want him to do well, and I think if he knows we are working together, I'm hopeful he will make improvements. Thank you so much for your time, you've been helpful; I'm sure we can get him on track and keep him there. If there are any questions or concerns, please don't hesitate to contact me. Take care."

Always watch your approach. Before calling, have your thoughts together and keep an outline similar to the script. Don't be a tattletale and state every single thing the student has done; it may reflect on your classroom management practices and backfire on you. A parent may also be disappointed to not hear about the situations you address sooner. Of course, you can explain that the last thing they did was the icing on the cake, so you felt it was imperative to contact them now to curb the behavior before it worsened. If it is small situation, it's water under the bridge. As you are on the phone take notes as needed. You won't be able to remember everything you discussed. If there are any parent concerns, listen.

Practical eMail Advice

Emailing is such a convenient way to communicate with parents. However, it can be printed and used for you or against you at any time. What we write and how we write is crucial in getting the message across as we intend. Wording is important. Avoid using all caps; it represents yelling. Reread your email before sending even if you have to walk away and return to the screen before pressing send. Keep a professional, appropriate tone, and edit for any grammatical errors. If the email from a parent has a grim tone, wait a day before responding to give a cooling-off period; it may be better to set up a face-to-face conference to address concerns. Keep emails brief and to the point. Don't elaborate and give details because what you mean does not mean it is received in the same manner.

When Contact Goes Bad

It is very possible that a phone call home or email can turn sour. The parent may become hostile and upset with you. If it is a phone call, your best bet is to stay quiet and don't react suddenly. We automatically want to go into defense mode, but meeting fire with fire is not wise. If the parent hasn't calmed down after while, do not just sit there on the phone and take it but respectfully remove yourself from the call. State sincerely, directly, and calmly, regardless if they continue to talk or not, "I am sorry that we are not able to come to a resolution. I want to talk further about your concern. I am going to hang up now and will be in contact." Inform administration immediately so they are aware of the situation. The parent may decide to come up to the school to further the conversation, or they may want to contact the school board. Either way, you want administration to know what has occurred. Allow administration to take it from there and advise you on the next steps. In the same way, if a parent sends or is responding to an email in a hostile way, don't respond with an email. Either call them, because sometimes a call can smooth out the hostility and clear up any misunderstandings, or opt to seek assistance from administration.

In brief, parents play a vital role in their child's education. Whether you have an overly-involved parent or a non-attentive parent, don't let that distract you from your goal of making sure every child in your class is successful. There have been times where a parent and I did not have the most pleasant interaction; however, I treated the child as I would any other one of my students. Don't take your frustration out on the student. It is true that we have the "power of the pen," but don't let negative parent encounters influence the ethical decisions of assigning grades or building a relationship.

Closing Remarks: The Real

Teachers undoubtedly have a difficult job to do. We are not recognized for all the work that goes into educating the whole child. We wear many hats, many that we didn't intentionally sign up for, but we are charged with wearing all hats, and well! You matter to students. How you treat them, how you teach them, the words you say, how you behave; they are looking. What do you want to be remembered by? Often, I sit and reminisce about my school days. I have memorable moments with old school buddies about being in Mr. or Ms. So and So's class. I remember a teacher falling asleep in class, another explaining to students how certain drugs were made; I remember one who yelled so much that everyone was terrified to breathe in her class. I can also recall the ones that inspired me beyond measure, and instead of asking me what I wanted to be, they made me think about what type of person I wanted to become. What will be your legacy? Treat your students as you would want to be treated. Don't label students and speak negative words over their lives. We are a key component in their lives. We hold so much power in building them up and keeping them safe from what the world throws at them. If you were a student, would you want to be in your class? Would you want your own children or loved ones in your classroom? Teachers touch the lives of thousands; our influence goes beyond measure. Therefore, be an educator that other educators would want to mimic. I hope these few words find you well!

Further Suggested Reading

Gregory, Gayle. (2008) Differentiated Instructional Strategies in Practice. Thousand Oaks, Ca:. Corwin Press

Gurian, Michael, Stevens, Kathy, King, Kelley. Strategies for Teaching Boys and Girls, 2008. Jossey-Bass Teacher

Hammond, Zaretta, Culturally Responsive Teaching and the Brain: Promoting Authentic Engagement and Rigor among Culturally and Linguistically Diverse Students

Lindsey, D. & R., Martinez, R. Culturally Proficient Coaching. Thousand Oaks, Ca: 2007. Corwin Press.

Lindscy, D. & R., Martincz, R. Culturally Proficient Learning Communities. Thousand Oaks, Ca: 2009 Thousand Oaks, Ca: 2007. Corwin Press.

Tatum, B. (2003). Why are all the Black kids sitting together in the cafeteria? A psychologist explains the development of racial identity. New York: Basic Books.

Tilton, L. (2003). The teacher's toolbox for differentiating instruction: 700 strategies, tips, tools, and techniques. Shorewood, MN: Covington Cove Publications.

Yisreal, Sean. Classroom Management: A Guide for Urban School Teachers

Yisreal, Sean. Cleopatra Teacher Rules: Effective Strategies for Engaging Students and Increasing Achievement

Yisreal, Sean. The Urban Teacher's Guide to Classroom Management

Warren, S. R. 2002. Stories from the classroom: How expectations and efficacy of diverse teachers affect the academic performance of children in poor urban schools. Educational Horizons 80(3): 109–16.

Bibliography

Aikens, N. L., & Barbarin, O. (2008). Socioeconomic differences in reading trajectories: The contribution of family, neighborhood, and school contexts. Journal of Educational Psychology, 100, 235-251.

Ballou, H. (2001, June 9). Decide to think big—Expect big results. The Transformational Leadership Strategist. Retrieved from http://transformationalstrategist.com/decide-to-think-big-expect-big- results/

Brown-Jeffy, S., and J. Cooper. 2011. Toward a conceptual framework of culturally relevant pedagogy: An overview of the conceptual and theoretical literature. Teacher Education Quarterly 38 (1): 65–84.

Canter, L. (1997). Behavior management: Keeping up with the times. Learning, 25 (4), 28-34.

Cartledge, G., & Lo, Y. (2006). Teaching urban learners: Culturally responsive strategies for developing academic and behavioral competence. Champaign, IL: Research Press.

Classroom Management: Training Our Future Teachers, (January 2014), National Council on Teacher Quality, Baltimore, MD.

Corso, M, Bundick, M., Quaglia, R., & Haywood, D. (2013) Where student, teacher, and content meet: Student engagement in the secondary school classroom. American Secondary Education (41) 3. 50-61.

Cushman, P. 2005. "It's Just Not a Real Bloke's Job: Male Teachers in the Primary School." Asia-Pacific Journal of Teacher Education 33 (3): 321–338.

http://www.edutopia.org/pdfs/resources/wiggins-mctigh e-backward-design-why-backward-is-best.pdf Grant Wiggins and Jay McTighe

Daft, R. L. (2008). The leadership experience (4th ed.). Mason, OH: SouthWestern.

Davis-Kean, P. E. (2005). The influence of parent education and family income on child achievement: The indirect role of parental expectations and the home environment. Journal of Family Psychology, 19(2), 294-304.

Duke, N. K., and P. D. Pearson, "Effective Practices for Developing Reading Comprehension," in A. E. Farstup & S. J. Samuels (eds.), What Research has to Say About Reading Instruction, International Reading Association, Newark, Delaware, 2002, pp. 205-242.

Duplass J. (2006). Middle and High School Teaching: Methods, Standards, and Best Practices. Boston: Houghton Mifflin Company. p. 204.

Ellerbrock, Cheryl R., Bridget Abbas, Michael DiCicco, Jennifer M. Denmon, Laura Sabella, and Jennifer Hart: Relationships: The fundamental R in education May 2015 Sage Publication Kappen Magazine

Epstein, J., Sanders, M., Simon, B., Salinas, K., Jansorn, N., Van Voorhis, F. (2002). School, family, and community partnerships: Your handbook for action (2nd ed.). Thousand Oaks, CA: Corwin Press.

Esptein, J. L. (1992). School and family partnerships. In M. Aiken (Ed.), Encyclopedia of Educational Research (6th, pp. 1139-1151). New York: MacMillan.

Evans, M. D., Kelley, J., Sikora, J., & Treiman, D. J. (2010). Family scholarly culture and educational success: Books and schooling in 27 nations. Research in Social Stratification and Mobility, 28(2), 171-197.

Evertson, C. M., Emmer, E. T., & Worsham, M. E. (2006). Classroom management for elementary teachers (7th ed.). Boston, MA: Pearson Allyn & Bacon.

Fink, D. L. (2005). Integrated course design. Manhattan, KS: The IDEA Center.

Retrieved from August 2015 http://ideaedu.org/wpcontent/uploads/2014/11/Idea_Paper_42.pdf

Fisher, D., & Frey, N. (2007). Checking for understanding: Formative assessment techniques for your classroom. Alexandria, VA: ASCD.

Gay, G. 2000. Culturally responsive teaching: Theory, research, and practice. New York: Teachers College Press.

Gay, G., & Howard, T. C. (2000). Multicultural teacher education for the 21st century. The Teacher Educator, 36(1), 1-16.

Glasser, W. (1998). Choice theory. New York: Harper Collins.

Greenstein, Laura, What Teachers Really Need to Know about Formative Assessment. Alexandria, Virginia: Association for Supervision & Curriculum Development, 2010.

Greenwood, C. R., Horton, B. T., & Utley, C. A. (2002). Academic engagement: Current perspectives on research and practice. School Psychology Review, 31, 328–349.

Heritage, M. (2008). Learning progressions: Supporting instruction and formative assessment. University of California, CA: Graduate School of Education and Information Studies.

Hess, K. (2008). Learning progressions in K-8 classrooms: How progress maps can influence classroom practice and perceptions and help teachers make more informed instructional decisions in support of struggling learners. Minneapolis, MN: National Center on Educational Outcomes.

Hill, N. E., & Tyson, D. F. (2009). Parental involvement in middle school: A meta-analytic assessment of the strategies that promote achievement. Developmental Psychology, 45, 740–763.

Hogan, R., & Kaiser, R. B. (2005). What We Know about Leadership. Review of General Psychology, 9(2), 169.

Ingersoll, R. & May, H. (2011). Recruitment, retention, and the minority teacher shortage. Philadelphia, PA: Consortium for Policy Research in Education, University of Pennsylvania and Center for Educational Research in the Interest of Underserved Students, University of California, Santa Cruz.

Johnson, J. F., Perez, L. G., & Uline, C. L. (2012). Teaching practices from America's best urban schools: A guide for school and classroom leaders. New York: Routledge.

Kauffman, D., Johnson, S. M., Kardos, S. M., Liu, E., & Peske, H. G. (2002). "Lost at sea": New teachers' experiences with curriculum and assessment. Teachers College Record, 104(2), 273–300.

Kohl, Gwynne O., Liliana J. Lengua, and Robert J. McMahon. 2000. "Parent Involvement in School Conceptualizing Multiple Dimensions and Their Relations with Family and Demographic Risk Factors." Journal of School Psychology 38 (6): 501–523.

Ladson-Billings, G. (2009). The dream-keepers: Successful teachers of African American children. San Francisco, CA: Jossey-Bass.

Lane, K., Carter, W., Pierson, M., & Glaeser, B. (2006). Academic, social, and behavioral characteristics of high school students with emotional disturbances or learning disabilities. Journal of Emotional & Behavioral Disorders, 14 (2), 108-117.

Lee, V. E. & Burkam, D. T. (2002). Inequality at the starting gate: Social background differences in achievement as children begin school. Washington, D.C.: Economic Policy Institute.

Leithwood, K, Begley, P. T, & Cousins, J.B. (1994). Developing expert leadership for future schools. London: Falmer.

"Lesson Planning" Research Starters eNotes.com, Inc. eNotes.com 24 May 2016 <http://www.enotes.com/research-starters/lesson-planning#research-starter-research-starter>

Marzano, R. J. (2003). What works in schools: Translating research into action. Alexandria, VA: ASCD.

Merritt, E.G., Wanless, S.B., Rimm-Kaufman, S.E., Cameron, C., James L., & Peugh, J. L. (2012). The contribution of teachers' emotional support to children's social behaviors and self-regulatory skills in first grade. School Psychology Review, 41(2), 141–159.

Milner, H. R. (2010). Start where you are, but don't stay there: Understanding diversity, opportunity gaps, and teaching in today's classrooms. Cambridge, MA: Harvard Education Press.

Morgan, P. L., Farkas, G., Hillemeier, M. M., & Maczuga, S. (2009). Risk factors for learning-related behavior problems at 24 months of age: Population-based estimates. Journal of Abnormal Child Psychology, 37, 401-413.

Marzano's What Works in Schools: Translating Research into Action (2003) and School Leadership That Works (2005) presents research that identifies factors at the school (and district) level that have a positive impact on student achievement.

McTighe, J., & Wiggins, G. (1999). Understanding by Design professional development workbook. Alexandria, VA: ASCD.

McTighe, J., & Wiggins, G. (2006). Understanding by Design (2nd Ed.), Pearson Education, Inc. Upper Saddle River, NJ.]

Moll, L. C., Amanti, C., Neff, D., & Gonzalez, N. (1992). Funds of knowledge for teaching: Using a qualitative approach to connect homes and classrooms. Theory Into Practice, 31(2), 132-141.

National Education Association. 2011. Transforming Teaching: Connecting Professional Responsibility with Student Learning. Washington, DC: Author.

Newman, R. (2013). Teaching and Learning in the 21st Century: Connecting the Dots. San Diego, CA: Bridgepoint Education Inc.

Nieto, S. (1996). Affirming diversity: The sociopolitical context of multicultural education (2nd ed.). White Plains, NY: Longman.

Noddings, N. (2005). The challenge to care in schools: An alternative approach to education (2nd ed.). New York, NY: Teachers College Press. In caring classroom communities, care is reciprocal; those who care ultimately are also cared for.

Northeast and Islands Regional Educational Laboratory at Brown University (LAB). (2002).

The diversity kit: An introductory resource for social change in education. Providence, RI: Brown University. Available: http://www.alliance.brown.edu/tdl/diversitykit.shtml

Northouse, P. G. (2010). Leadership: Theory and practice, 5th ed. Los Angeles, CA: Sage.

Oliver, R. M., Wehby, J. H., Reschly, D. J. (2011, June). Teacher classroom management practices: Effects on disruptive or aggressive student behavior. Retrieved on April 2, 2016, from http://www.campbellcollaboration.org/news_/Classroom_management_versus_problem_behavior.php

Padron, Y. N., Waxman, H. C., and Rivera, H. H. (2002). Educating Hispanic students: Effective instructional practices (Practitioner Brief #5).

Raikes, H., Pan, B.A., Luze, G.J., Tamis-LeMonda, C.S., Brooks-Gunn, J., Constantine, J., Tarullo, L.B., Raikes, H.A., Rodriguez, E. (2006). "Mother-child book reading in low-income families: Correlates and outcomes during the first three years of life." Child Development, 77(4).

Sakiz, G., Pape S.J., & Woolfolk Hoy, A. (2012). Does perceived teacher affective support matter for middle school students in mathematics classrooms? Journal of School Psychology, 50, 235–255.

Scott, T.M., Nelson, C.M., & Liaupsin, C. (2001). Effective instruction: The forgotten component in preventing school violence. Education and Treatment of Children, 24, 309-322. This article originally appeared in the September/October 2011 issue of TEC Kristin L. Sayeski and Monica R. Brown

Sheets, R. (1999). Relating competence in an urban classroom to ethnic identity development. In R. Sheets (Ed.), Racial and ethnic identity in school practices: Aspects of human development. Mahwah, NJ: Lawrence Erlbaum Associates.

Sparks, S.D., "Study Finds Gaps Remain Large for Hispanic Students," Education Week, June 23, 2011.

Stiggins, R. J., Arter, J. A., Chappuis, J., & Chappuis, S. (2004). Classroom assessment for student learning: Doing it right—using it well. Portland, OR: Assessment Training Institute

Sylwester, Robert, The Adolescent Brain: Reaching for Autonomy, Corwin Press, 2007

Tomlinson, C., & Imbeau, M. (2010). Leading and managing a differentiated classroom. Alexandria, VA: ASCD.

Tomlinson, C. A. (August 2000). Differentiation of Instruction in the Elementary Grades. ERIC Digest. ERIC Clearinghouse on Elementary and Early Childhood Education.,

B. M., Thomas, E., Drago, K., & Rex, L. A. (2013). Examining studies of inquiry-based learning in three fields of education: Sparking generative conversation. Journal of Teacher Education, 64(5), 387-408

Tomlinson, C. (1996). Differentiating instruction for mixed-ability classrooms [A professional inquiry kit]. Alexandria, VA: Association for Supervision and Curriculum Development.

U.S. Department of Education, National Center for Education Statistics. (2016). Digest of Education Statistics, 2015 (NCES 2016-014).

Viadero, D., "Scholars Probe Diverse Effects of Exit Exams," Education Week, April 29, 2009.

Viadero, D., "Lags in Minority Achievement Defy Traditional Explanations," Education Week, March 22, 2000.

Villegas, A. M. (1991). Culturally responsive pedagogy for the 1990's and beyond. Washington, DC: ERIC Clearinghouse on Teacher Education

Vincent The Multigrade Classroom: A Resource Handbook for Small, Rural Schools Susan Vincent, Editor

Wang, & Walberg (2004). Building Academic Success on Social and Emotional Learning (SEL): What Does the Research Say?

Weinstein, C., S. Tomlinson-Clark, and M. Curran. 2004. Toward a conception of culturally responsive classroom management. Journal of Teacher Education 55 (1): 25–38.

Wentzel, K. R., Battle, A., Russell, S. L., & Looney, L. B. (2010). Social supports from teachers and peers as predictors of academic and social motivation. Contemporary Educational Psychology, 35(3), 193-202.

Wiggens, G., & McTighe, J. (2005). Understanding by Design. Expanded 2nd Edition. Alexandria, VA: Association for the Supervision and Curriculum Development. ED553616.

Wiggins, G. P., & McTighe, J. (2005). Understanding by design (Expanded 2nd ed.). Upper Saddle River, NJ: Pearson Education.

Womack, S. T., Pepper, S., Hanna, S. L., & Bell, C. D. (2015, February). Most Effective Practices in Lesson Planning. Retrieved from http://files.eric.ed.gov/fulltext/

Winston, B. (2002). Be a leader for God's sake. Virginia Beach, VA: Regent University School of Leadership Studies.

Weiss, R.P. "Emotion and Learning." Training & Development 54, no. 11 (2000): 45

www.ingramcontent.com/pod-product-compliance
Lightning Source LLC
Chambersburg PA
CBHW051359290426
44108CB00015B/2088